Production of the 'Self' in the Digital Age

Yasmin Ibrahim

Production of the 'Self' in the Digital Age

palgrave
macmillan

Yasmin Ibrahim
School of Business and Management
Queen Mary University of London
London, UK

ISBN 978-3-030-08991-7   ISBN 978-3-319-74436-0   (eBook)
https://doi.org/10.1007/978-3-319-74436-0

This Palgrave Macmillan imprint is published by Springer Nature
The registered company is Springer International Publishing AG
The registered company address is: Gewerbestrasse 11, 6330 Cham, Switzerland

To Khalil.
For the invaluable work you
do to save lives
and improve women's health.

PREFACE

The story of the self entwined with digital media platforms and imaging technologies in the digital age is one that is still unfolding in all its nuanced complexities. The self as a form of value entangled with the back operations of the web is implicated in both value creation and as content and commodity for mass and niche consuming audiences. Amidst these opportunities to be part of value creation and commodification, the self remains deeply aestheticized and consumed in its everyday settings. In the banal richness of the everyday, it performs to new forms of gaze and consuming publics curious of the other and curious in the other. The desire to see ourselves being validated and consumed by others facilitates a whole new economy where the self is rebirthed through new mediated platforms where sharing and community endorsements make the solitary self a form of transaction. New vulnerabilities emerge as do new forms of self-expression. The objectification of the self in the digital age invites a whole array of introspection into self production through immaterial platforms where the self acquires new means to be exchanged and to acquire value. These are intrinsic to the digital age where self-production entails renewed engagement with everyday technologies that claim the body as a site for embedding. The corporealisation of technology in our everyday lives means that ubiquitous computing and imaging constantly graze the body inviting it to be part of the landscape of production in the digital age. In these technological engagements, the self is expressed through the sharing platforms that aestheticize the self and its everyday life as means to diarise its journeys, validate its presence and to review its deep seated anxieties with mortality and find mechanisms for immortality. The currency of the 'selfie' isn't just a story about convergence of technologies or the incorporation of these in our smartphones or indeed the extension of our senses through wearable technologies. The 'selfie' is about our strategies to re-enact the self through new modes of expression, new modes of living and new modes of co-presence with others while enabling a means to view ourselves through the screen. This re-imagination of the self through modes of immateriality while seeking to extend our mortality through the virality and immortality of the screen conveys the complex interplay of tensions in the digital age where our disembodied presence online and its constant anxieties with death and elongation of mortality carve out strategies to commodify and aestheticize the self through and with the screen. The self on the screen will remain a primal moment of fascination today and for time to come.

London, UK   Yasmin Ibrahim

Acknowledgements

Chapter 2
This chapter is derived in part from an article published in *Politics, Protest and Empowerment in Digital Spaces*, published in December 2016, IGI copyright, reprinted by permission. DOI: 10.4018/978-1-5225-1862-4.

Chapter 3
This chapter is derived in part from an article published in *Collaborative Technologies and Applications for Interactive Information Design: Emerging Trends in User Experiences: Emerging Trends in User Experiences*, published in December 2009, IGI copyright, reprinted by permission. DOI: 10.4018/978-1-60566-727-0.

CONTENTS

CHAPTER 1

Producing the 'Self' Online. Self and Its Relationship with the Screen and Mirror

Abstract The insertion of our lives into the screen and fascination with the screen represent moments of extreme curiosity and primal interest with this self-as-part-of-the-human condition. This introductory chapter argues that this 'infantile' moment of self-discovery with the screen is equivalent to the mirror moment of self-identification. In the digital age, the screen performs a multitude of functions from self-discovery to voyeurism, encapsulating our renewed ubiquitous fascination with the mirror as the starting point of self-discovery. Our obsession with the screen in the digital age needs to be located as a cultural artefact associated with news, celebrity and the spectacular. In the digital age, the screen and mirror become interchangeable as they become part of the project to perform, project and consume the self. This introductory chapter examines the production of the self in the digital age through its troubled and unsettling relationship with the mirror and the screen as artefacts of self-production.

Keywords Mirror • Screen • Self-image • Self-representation • Self-construction

INTRODUCTION

In the digital age, the self remains a primal subject of interest with our increasing immersion into a pervasive screen culture. Today we have an incestuous bind with the screen as a cultural artefact that has been domesticated into our everyday lives over time and invoked as a medium for

© The Author(s) 2018

Y. Ibrahim, *Production of the 'Self' in the Digital Age*,
https://doi.org/10.1007/978-3-319-74436-0_1

1

voyeurism and pleasure-seeking. Where the screen once stood for the construction of a wider world beyond us, today it is a theatre for assembling ourselves and narrating our lived moments to others. By premising the notions of mirror and screen in this introductory chapter, I examine how the mirror and screen coalesce in the construction of the self in the digital self. This digital-screen self is a self that is made vulnerable through its screening yet a self that is constantly mesmerised by its own image online. It represents a potent moment in the digital age. Where the mirror and screen become one is the project of the self in its journey of self-discovery.

Historically, the mirror has been intimately linked to the composition of the self. In the late fourteenth and fifteenth centuries in Florence, Italy, there was a proliferation of texts that discussed the mirror with painting, including self-portraits (see Yiu 2005). More specifically, as Yiu (2005: 189–209) points out, the 'two earliest references to the mirror and painting in Renaissance texts both date from the fourteenth century and mention the mirror in conjunction with self-portraiture. In fact, the mirror was intimately associated with major innovations such as naturalistic representation particularly the realistic self-portrait'.

In this age of the screen, our notions of what is private and public become redefined, as we offer ourselves as commodities for the consumption of others. With the convergence of technologies, we are able constantly to record and capture ourselves on the move, making the self both a subject and an object of production and consumption online. These seamless interplays between production, commodification and consumption mean that the self is not just endlessly constructed but curated through the screen. The banality of the everyday, and equally the mix of life experiences of the self, bind the ordinary with the perfunctory, entwining both the ordinary and extraordinary into narrations of the self online. As such, the digital architecture performs to the politics of the self where the convergence of technologies, the shifting realms of private and public, and also our engagement with an image-laden world anchor self-curation as a vital part of digital living. The self as a complex entity that can be performed, curated, produced and consumed makes the self an open-ended project in the digital age. Unfinished, non-unitary and absorbed through a digital architecture as bits and bytes.

While there is certainly an intense fascination with the self and its modes of visibility online (see Ibrahim 2011), it would be reductionist to consign self-curation solely into the ambit of narcissistic tendencies. New media technologies and their appropriation into our everyday lives has created an intimacy with technologies where these have become an extension of our senses, slowly integrating into our bodily bio-rhythms as sensory organs. The self performed and visualised through the screen, and equally coded as data through tracking technologies, metrics and algorithms, reveals the complexity of identity creation and performance in this cyber culture. Our everyday interactions recoded as data online can be about the creation of both social capital and new forms of vulnerabilities. The ubiquitous regeneration of the self through the new data economy and image-capture technologies means the self is reconfigured and redistributed through digital bytes. This can be interpreted as the loss 'aura' (Benjamin 1995) with the self being reassembled and recirculated through new media platforms. The transference of the physical body into digital modes of representation means that something is compromised through this digital resurrection where the flesh is transformed into bytes and where it is amenable to a politics of 'virality'. This commodification of the self is a resonant part of digital living and self-representation today and as such it is less preoccupied with the loss of aura or the compromise of its corporeal matter, instead yielding to the accumulation of social capital online where it offers itself as a commodity through the gaze of unknown others.

The screen predates this digital age both historically and culturally in terms of our fascination and obsession with it. Most societies have a deep resonance with the screen for the modes of escape and fantasies it offers. The screen is symbolic of worlds beyond us and equally for locating us within it. We recognise its ability to be unceasing in the production of the spectacle and its unbounded imagination. The celluloid screen is pregnant with desire and the unattainable, delivering distance and transporting us back and forth in time. The screen in modernity is made manifest through television, cinema, theatre, advertising billboards, smartphones and mobile devices that thwart the reality of our immediate environments. When broadcasting as a form of mass mediation entered our homes, it sought to domesticate our senses: our notions of proximity and distance. Locating itself in the heart of our habitat, television claimed our sense of reality and representation, offering a sensorium into the outer world, transporting us into distant realms without us leaving the confines of our homes. With the passage of time, mobile and ambient technologies targeted the body, seeking to colonise its senses and functions by locating these onto the corporeal body. The corporealisation of mobile technologies lay siege to not just our sense of self but our innate desires to be part of the screen and to be re-birthed through these. Mass mediated technologies gave way to mobile gadgets, which sought to personalise pleasure, to carve out a solitary state while thrusting us into new modes of interactively without de-centring the self. The transcendence from the domestication of technologies to their corporealisation meant that the self became initiated into a culture of the 'self watching the self' where we could be projected onto the screen as well as inserted into the screen. Like the mirror, the screen acquired an autoscopic device immersed in the politics of self-identification and objectification through the gaze of others.

In the age of convergence and digital culture, the self transacted as a commodity online is a controversial entity, seeking to build and consolidate its presence while bound through the workings of capital online. The complicit nature of this self-commodification through commercial platforms and social networking sites means that the economy of self-production online is one that works to a capitalist agenda where every form of creative, artistic and voluntary endeavour can be monetised by a data economy for filling vast swathes of the digital realm with user-generated content (UGC). Everything becomes touched by capital without foreclosing anything as sacred or private. The commodification of the self in this era of extreme self-curation and its co-mingling with capital symbolises exploitation of the human self and spirit while asserting a rhetoric of empowerment where the screen is presented as a democratising force for all. Critical readings on the exploitation of capital online point to the new media environment seducing and extracting new forms of labour, which yield value for marketers and commercial advertisers by leveraging on the creative agency of the consumer (see Bonsu and Darmody 2008: 365; Terranova 2000). The extraction of surplus immaterial labour from user-generated platforms through notions of co-creation rebirths the self as a material and cultural artefact in the new media economy. The self in the digital age is a complicit entity in terms of self-objectification, value creation and exploitation meandering through social networking sites that claim it as content and data. With the self as a cultural artefact in these new and emergent forms of consumerism online, capital inscribes the 'digital self' as part of its imperative to release value and data relentlessly. The self as a material artefact online is part of the violence that capital unleashes as it constantly draws on our fascination with our mirror and screen image as human flaws that can be exploited (Ibrahim 2008a, 2009). If the internet seduced us into recasting our pets as performing animals for the pleasure of others, the self is no exception in this performance and monetisation economy.

The proliferation of profile culture and the 'selfie' generation that underpin these practices of self-curation and aestheticization is increasingly viewed as part of an emergent narcissistic culture in postmodernity.

The ancient tragic tale of Narcissus provides a moral caution for humanity. It reveals the mortal flaw of our primal fascinations with ourselves. Narcissus' insatiable obsession with his own reflection is seen as Western civilisation's madness of self-obsession unleashed in our quest for self-knowledge (Davies 1989: 265). The unrelenting quest for uniqueness and individuation can be self-destructive for humanity if left unchecked. The screen as the mirror in the online environment brings the tale of Narcissus into renewed focus, showcasing human frailties in the digital age where we constantly consume and monitor our digital selves online.

The virtual world and the attendant technologies to construct and project the self are then associated with new forms of vulnerabilities and anxieties, making the 'project of the self' an unstable and exacting enterprise online. Self-love is seen as inducing self-destruction and madness, highlighting the fatal flaw in the human condition. The digital economy then straddles the destructive and exploitative where new forms of expressions of the self rekindle our obsession with our own reflection. While discourses of UGC have been closely associated with empowerment and agency, what is less theorised is how capital exploits our self-love as an intrinsic logic to elicit content and interactions, thrusting the self into new ambits of self-consumerism and voyeurism. Capital's enterprise with self-fetishisation and the interplay between the two in the digital economy is an important aspect of digital living but one that has not received adequate scholarship in the field. Notwithstanding the vulnerabilities of the human condition in new media platforms, self-curation can be anchored beyond capital's exploitative tendencies. The potential for therapeutic benefits through new modes of self-expression and validation through communal gaze also need to be acknowledged.

Social media sites exploit the 'social' as they enable us to transact and interact through a profile culture and an architecture of interactivity where the self is visualised through its engagements and movements. As such, new media scholarship has reviewed the constitution of the self in the virtual sphere through interactive modes of communication where the screen becomes domesticated into our everyday lives (see Turkle 1995; Lev Manovich 2001; Bolter and Grusin 2000). These platforms then function as 'technologies of the self' premising on modes of identity creation and self-objectification. Social networking sites as facilities for self-presentation and identity negotiation enmesh public and private spaces with multiple audiences, enabling a networked self to emerge (Papacharissi 2011: 304–305). With the emergence of new media technologies, the self has been tightly implicated with these mediated platforms, particularly the screen where it is closely related with identity politics online. We become subjects and objects that play out our intimate and cultural identities online (Bolter and Grusin 2000: 232). The internet as a social laboratory for identity creation and relationship formation facilitates the refashioning of the self and is emblematic of postmodernity, according to Sherry Turkle (1995: 180). In reiterating this, Le Manovich (2001: 94) contends that the 'society of the screen' has substituted the 'society of spectacle' making it omnipresent and perfunctory. This screen society is equally one in which the embodied self is characterised by a malleable cyber self defined through its fluidity (Rocamora 2011). In examining blogs as spaces for identity construction and representations of femininity, Agnès Rocamora (2011: 416) transposes the screen as a mirror for women as specular entities where 'new technologies have enabled digital screens to look at oneself' like a mirror.

The metaphors of the mirror and screen as artefacts of the ocular, perform as sites for our insatiable appetite to consume ourselves. This chapter emphasises the importance of the self in the virtual realm where humanity is constantly engaged with technology. New technologies as a site of fervent human activity also underscore these as 'technologies of the self' where it is tightly entwined with the 'social' on social media as well as the generativity of UGC where we are bound through networked assemblages. Within both the mirror and screen are reflective and projective qualities providing a canvas to expand the politics of self-objectification and its primal fascination with itself. Drawing on the notion of the 'mirror phase' as a significant milestone for human development, this chapter colocates this moment of discovery with society's incestuous relationship with screen culture as a form of socialisation into a wider world. In doing so, it asserts that modern society has a primal relationship with the mirror and screen in the digital age where these coalesce as an elongated project of self-construction.

Self and Its Digital Genesis

Philosophical enquiry through time has been saturated with metaphysical questions about whether we really exist and is consciousness a Cartesian duality which separates mind and body. We have also sought to locate consciousness and the existence of human presence through the study of sentiments and emotions. Within a given environment, the subjective feeling of existence is defined as presence and where it is mediated through technology it is referred to as telepresence (see Heeter 1992; Sheridan 1992; Steuer 1992). In contrast, existence can be imbricated through our normal everyday physical environment (see Heidegger 1962). Through the concept of 'enframement' Heidegger (1972) posits technology as something external yet generative from human agency, though divorced from human body and its substance. J.J. Gibson perceives existence through the reciprocal and entwined relationship between the self and the environment. As humans suspended in our environment, we perceive objects and events but simultaneously our position and motion are derived through their co-location (Bahrick et al. 1996: 191). The concept of existence is quite central in the realm of virtual reality where this reality is forged through a relationship between physical and psychological domains (Minsky 1980). Technology matters for the ways in which it can enter our modes of existence and its ability to tamper with our senses, exerting new forms of anxieties for humanity in the industrial, digital and post-digital age. Technology beyond imposing an external reality can re-order the embodied body and its senses. Our articulations of technological mutations such as the posthuman and cyborg are then birthed through these imaginations and anxieties where technology extracts and reframes the senses through its ubiquity and pervasiveness (Pasek 2014). Technology's ability to mediate our affective states builds the screen as a potent platform of disembodied presence.

Our conceptualisation of the virtual world and notions of disembodied presence further complicate the notion of existence online. We speak of online and offline as bounded spheres but in reality these worlds are enmeshed in complex ways. As unbounded spheres, veering between offline and online modes and practices, our transactions and engagements increasingly premise our negotiation of identity and presence online. These can manifest as data, images, emoticons or profiles and cumulatively lend to a digital identity or a digital footprint. It underscores the significance of existence online and how these are mediated through existing social norms and through the creation of new modes of practice that emerge in new media platforms in our pervasive engagements with technology and the architecture of the internet (Ibrahim 2011, 2012).

Our digital presence online is infused through the politics of identity creation. With an immaterial and disembodied presence online, the politics of self is about a transcendence from material presence to forms of immateriality where we are inserted as disembodied entities on the screen. We are inserted into a screen where we can watch ourselves, leave traces, and be aware of others watching us, following us, tagging us. Like the mirror's potent moment of self-discovery, the screen is just as destabilising. Historically, the mirror unleashes a mystical quality beyond projecting our reflections, possessing supernatural powers to entrap souls and spirits in ancient folklores (Rochat and Zahavi 2011). Our relationship with the mirror is shaped through its mythical and mystical qualities, redolent with possibilities to contain potent and hidden powers even while it projects our self-image.

An infant's perception of the self has been theorised from different perspectives. One strand of scholarship argues that infants perceive a differentiated self from the start of their lives and as such possess an integrated knowledge on many fronts (see Gibson 1986; Bahrick 1995; Bahrick et al. 1996: 190). This means the self is perceived as a unique entity through the particularity of its physical attributes and this sense of differentiation intensifies over the period of human growth and development. This departs from the conventional assumption that the infant perceives the self as distinct over time (see Mahler and Furer 1968; Piaget 1954). For Jacques Lacan (2006) the mirror phase symbolises a moment of realisation for the infant of being a separate subject from others when it views the mirror reflection and recognises the image on the mirror as a self-reflection. The mirror phase is a primary construct and a significant milestone in human self-development and this potent moment of self-recognition provides a conceptual premise into self-understanding and development (Bahrick et al. 1996, 191).

In narrating the 'uncanny mirror and self-experience', Philippe Rochat and Dan Zahavi (2011) assert that the moment that the self experiences the mirror is an unsettling encounter across cultures and is deemed universal as it invokes an inextricable bind between humanity and its discovery of existence through this self-reflection. The reflection of oneself has a phantasmagoric quality, at once unsettling while drawing us into an unceasing awe with ourselves. Mirrors become objects of perpetual fascination in their ability to offer our reflections. While the discovery of the self is one of the most significant encounters of stimulation, the discovery of the 'mirror self' is an unstable mix of curiosity and fascination, but also anxiety (1996: 189).

Similarly, Merleau-Ponty (1964) concedes that the mirror moment of self-recognition is a turbulent moment of self-discovery. The visual representation through the reflection of the mirror for the child is also the very moment there is a recognition that the self can be objectified and extrapolated from the flesh of the body. The mirror then stands for a dawning moment of realisation providing the possibility to apprehend the body as a delineated object where the child sees herself as others see her. This dawning moment of the image as part of the self is also about the uncoupling of the body from its visual representation (Rochat and Zahavi 2011).

The mirror moment for Lacan, symbolises transcendence from the real person to the experiencing of the 'imaginary self' through mirror image, abstracted from the real self. This moment is both about alienation and viewing oneself as a commodity extracted from the self. The mirror moment is then about the birth of an objectified self. The gaze of the others and their consumption of this entity works to pull the self from being situated through the embodied self (Merleau-Ponty 1964: 136). This moment of discovery or realisation that the self has an external dimension which can be consumed by others is disconcerting as the self is both exposed and commodified. The moment is marked through the alienation of the self in witnessing and experiencing the specular double (Rochat and Zahavi 2011: 6). Lacan's mirror stage is perceived as the arrival of the ego and the invocation of narcissistic tendencies in humans (Gallop 1982). The obsession with an image of the self constitutes narcissism and the mirror moment offers this encounter through our encounter with our own self-image.

The 'mirror moment' of self-discovery and unsettling realisation finds a longer frame of reference in the virtual environment. The online environment functions as a space for identity formation and creation but equally it coalesces the enigmatic qualities of the screen with the mirror. The screen as emblematic of fantasies and the unattainable combines with the awe produced by the mirror with our reflections. With the screen representing escape and obsession with the spectacular, it adds further complexity to our engagements online where the online world opens up immersive platforms where the self can be re-fashioned and where the corporeal body is disaggregated through the digital environment.

The televisual screen of broadcasting and big screens of cinema, which predate the internet, are portals to another world. A world of public spectacle, national amusement and teleportation into spaces beyond our immediate environment. The sort of 'mobile privatisation', which Raymond Williams (1974) accords to television, is a potent force in its ability to transport our mind and senses beyond our living rooms. If broadcasting as a form of national presence socialised the masses in according a veneration to the screen and its ability to play with our senses, new mobile technologies seduce us into private pleasures away from the communal consumption of television into celebrating solitary indulgence. This has further glorified the self as an individual through its ability to privatise the screen and to customise its relationship with it.

The screen as a site for pleasure and meaning-making also harks to an age of privatisation of technologies such that an intimate relationship develops with mobile technologies that locate the body, multiplying its senses through the screen. This 'intimatisation' of the screen where it is embedded to our body and senses means that technology is no longer 'enframed' or externalised as Heidegger contended. In effect, as Nicholas Negroponte (1995) prophesied, its embedding onto the mobile body substitutes our senses. Saturated with a richness of information and a persistent onslaught on its senses, the nervous system of the human has to contend with more than it is capable of in receiving or handling this ceaseless relay of stimuli and information. With the intimatisation of technologies, the self is resurrected as a performing entity in an age of information overload where the screen targets the body as a cognitive and affective entity. The emergence of a digital self is seen as a 'second self' (Turkle 2005) configuring these technologies as not just intimate but also remediating the relationship between the self and the machine. This notion of the 'second self' then dispels the myth that the self is a unitary self, and in the age of the internet it can equally acquire a multitude of presences where it can be reframed through its screen presence.

The screen as a part of our private and intimate realm or pleasure and leisure means that it also reassembles our notions of time and space. Where the television screen represented a national time through broadcasting, the intimate screen reconfigures the sense of time and space for the self as selective modes of solitude and personalisation afforded through mobile technologies. The advent of the Walkman repositioned the notion of domestication of technologies as portable, mobile and embedded onto the body. It symbolised the corporealisation of technologies, extending our senses and pleasures through the mobility of technologies and their co-location with the human body. It represented new forms of subjectivity through our relationships with technology, with the ability to double our vision, expand our memory, and to morph our senses.

Similarly, while portable devices such as handheld cameras and imaging technologies witnessed an intense capture and distribution of the self through photographs and home movies, the insertion of the self into the screen signified another form of consciousness. The facility to insert ourselves into a screen and to invite the gaze of others through the architecture of the web and UGC as well as interactive social media platforms is a significant moment for humanity. This is the precise moment where the mirror becomes the screen—an intense moment of awe, which can be offered to a wider audience. A screen culture in which the self can be commodified and aestheticized by others.

The concept of the 'gaze' in film theory as conceptualised by Laura Mulvey (1975) captures sexual and power relations through the act of consumption and commodification. It thrusts the politics of the screen into a duality of subject and object positions. In postmodernity, with the insertion of the self on the screen, there is coalescing of object and subject (Walker 2005). Jill Walker (2005: 184) contends that in the age of new media where we have the agency to represent ourselves, our fascination with reflections and shadows is about this emancipation and ability to abstract the self from generalisations of the mass media. As such in the virtual realm, the self is both subject and object.

Our ability to project the self is an indelible aspect of digital culture—where there is a genesis of a second self that acquires social capital through its performance. Its ability to exhibit itself to an unknown audience means it is in constant interplay with an interactive environment where it forges an intimate relationship with technology and its fluidity in terms of manifest forms online. The intertwining of these technologies, of self and its sense of aesthetics, morality and identity means that the self is constantly curated online. Self-curation enmeshes the complexities of the internet architecture, the corporealisation of mobile technologies and our unceasing primal fascination with the self as a project in postmodernity. The screen as a habitat for the digital self is then actively involved in impression management in terms of its everyday existence with and through the screen.

According to Jane Gallop (1982) the illusion of the mirror stage is that it introduces a fiction in the representation of the specular double where the body is constructed as a unified assemblage. This is in fact a moment of misrecognition or morphological distortion. Similarly, the transcendence of the body from the physical to the digital realm distorts the body (Pasek 2014). The normalisation of the digital image on screen means that we become uncritical about this technologically mediated self-construction. The screen for Pasek (2014), and our moments of self-recognition on it, are equally destabilising as bodies can be made alien or broken through visual transformation online. Rather than conceiving this technologically mediated visuality as dehumanising or dwarfed through the domination of technology, Pasek calls for these to be understood as perceptual introspection invoked by these technologies of the self. The digital self unlike the mirror self is re-configured constantly through technology and its fluidity.

THE MIRROR AND SCREEN IN CYBERSPACE

The screen and mirror project an illusion and have a capacity to distort. Both provide the possibilities to imagine and enter another paradigm of reality. In studies of child psychology and in human construction of religion, we often envisage and imagine other worlds beyond our physical world of existence. These imagined worlds as realms of unlimited possibilities, of new order and logic and even morality, stand in stark contrast to the reality of our own worlds. Lewis Carroll's *Alice in Wonderland* created another world in which the rules of the real world don't apply. Our positioning of the virtual as another realm in many ways captures our quest to imagine and create new worlds where the logic and order of the physical world can be subverted. The virtual becomes the playground for a hyperreality that seeks to immerse us through new norms and simulation. The casting of the self into this virtuality is also about the means to imagine and re-birth a new self not entirely crafted through the laws and logic of the physical world.

Cyberspace, in our initial imagination and hopes, was conceived as a space free from the capitalist agenda and a platform where we could be freed from our offline identities while being agile enough to traverse through these new realms of virtuality. It was imagined as a space freed from the governance of nations. Without being a form of afterlife premised in religions, the virtual provided a means to imagine a new world, rife with possibilities and providing 'consensual hallucination' (Gibson 1993) or a 'psychic theatre' (McDougall 1986) where our primal desires and fantasies can be unleashed. As such the self could be unlimited in its acquisition of avatars online where new forms of identities could emerge as morphed and relinquished from our offline identities. It meant we could straddle the possibilities in terms of identity politics from anonymity to multiple iterations, subverting the sense of a unitary self. As such the virtual world in our initial conceptualisations was fervent with possibilities and desires. Unlike the mortal world, where our identities could be obliterated through the inevitability of death, the virtual celebrated the ineradicable where matter and data can float ad infinitum.

From these earlier euphoric conceptions of the internet as a space of unmitigated re-invention, the emergence of social networking sites sought to bind our offline and online identities in complex ways, creating new forms of tension. Social networking sites put an undue emphasis on profile culture, encoding new forms of social capital through its connectivity and sociality with others. In contrast with our earlier endeavours to escape the mortal world through the virtual realm, this renewed emphasis on profile culture and the need to sustain the identity and presence of the self through its everyday activities and connectivity laid the emphasis on our endeavour to be in the world. These social networking sites also made image economies a resonant part of our virtual identities. As such, self-representation online became enacted through 'synchronous and asynchronous exhibitions on social media' (Hogan 2010: 377). The performative and exhibitionary online became new markers of identity in this exacting profile culture. Existence in these sites called for an active curation of the self online and our acute consciousness that the self is absorbed into a distributive and viral economy online where our presence and its representation could be torn from its context, given the architecture of the internet. As such social networking sites perform both as the screen and mirror on these sites as we consume ourselves while being cognitive of the gaze of others consuming us as commodities.

The obsession with the 'selfie' needs to be contextualized through this self-curation enabled by the technologies of the self. The acute objectification of the self is then also part of this enterprise. SNSs produce a reciprocal sociality in which the self is relentlessly traded with others and becomes an intrinsic aspect of the 'gift-giving' economy online. This sociality is also tightly enmeshed with the consumption and validation of a wider community (both known and unknown) on the internet. The self-exoticisation through the selfie elongates the project of the self online as it becomes part of a new visual vernacular of watching and aestheticizing the self. The self is marked through the banal of the everyday (see Ibrahim 2015) and equally through its forays into the unusual. As such the imaging of ourselves through the banal of the everyday provides a mechanism to narrate the self as a part of its lived reality and fiction, ensconcing the banal as a resonant aspect of our image economy online.

In postmodernity, while the advent of the internet was rife with possibilities and hope, the movement of capital, its colonisation of spaces and avarice to monetise and commodify matter meant content creation became a vital aspect of the online economy. UGC and processes such as co-creation, where users are voluntarily engaged in labour and enterprise from reviews to storytelling to knowledge creation, meant that the self and its activities online became a dynamic and productive aspect of this economy. The digital economy intrinsically valorises the self as a vivacious component of generativity where the self is unceasingly involved in offering itself as data and as a commodity, and in monitoring itself as part of the complex image economy and its attendant aesthetics. The facility to constantly publish, document and monitor ourselves as part of UGC means that the self is both an object and a subject online where it is immersed in the economy of providing immaterial labour while feeling empowered through its interactions and engagements with capital and networked relationships that project the self beyond its immediate realm. Capital, being cognitive of our primal fascination with the self, leverages on this obsession for self-discovery to extract labour and content. As such, capital exploits the flaws in the human condition and its insatiable appetite with itself. While our obsessions with the self can be exploited by the digital economy and its constant machinations to turn humans and their activities into data that can be traded with third parties for a multitude of reasons, the internet as a means to preserve the self and to generate new projects of the self in postmodernity should nevertheless be valued. The interplay of capital with the projects of the self cannot totally efface its agency or sense of self-empowerment made manifest through its digital engagements.

The mirror stage is defined as a turning point in human development as the subject visualises a totalising image of itself which has come from outside (Gallop 1982: 120). This totalising gaze of the mirror is nevertheless fragmented by the screen through its bits and bytes. If the mirror was responsible for presenting an entity abstracted from the flesh of the corporeal body, the screen has reassembled the body through data, imposing new forms of logic where the body is coded through external forces such as algorithms constituting the big data economy. As such, the body is data and becomes overloaded with data, as conceived by Nicholas Negroponte (1995) where the disembodied human is reconstituted not as flesh but data. The screen, like the mirror, represents a moment of fragmentation where the human is recoded through a data economy while decontextualized from its context and meaning (Ibrahim 2008b).

As we increasingly live our lives on the digital stage, we are constantly curating the self through our aesthetic modes, transforming the screen as a mirror projecting the self as a public entity that is performed and consumed in its digital manifestation. The mirror deeply entangled with self-representation, reflection of reality, self-discovery and desire remains a contentious space. The mirror is also entwined with truth and magic historically and hence it implicates self-construction as a problematic encounter where the notion of the unitary self fragments through its online and offline iterations but equally through its implication as data and content in the digital economy. The screen, as such, splinters the mirror image, extracting the self through the demands and presentational modes of the digital economy. The screen associated with simulacra, virtual reality and the ability to alter reality yet be mimetic is a space of unlimited possibilities to produce new environments and apparitions of us and others. The screen then becomes a space of new forms of anxieties and hopes but mostly constructions where the networked individual is re-imagined through new aesthetic modes as repositioned as a generative entity in a space where we constantly call others to attention, projecting the screen as a mirror. The self or the spectral body is then mired in illusion, remediated reality and new modes of aestheticization online. The flipping of the mirror into a screen signals our sustained interests in ourselves but also acute anxieties of producing the self online. As Vivian Schoback (1990) points out, the subject is reduced to a 'no-body' as electronic technology produces an evacuation of the sense of embodiment. This echoes a contention by Frederic Jameson (1998) that the confluence of capitalism with the social, political and economic has made it difficult for the subject to locate herself as a subject in history.

CONCLUSION

This chapter in utilising the notions of the screen and mirror examined the complex relationship the self has with its own image as a significant part of its self-development and discovery. Both mirror and screen as cultural artefacts have a long history with the development of the self both in terms of psychological growth but equally in the construction of reality of the outer world. The 'mirror moment' of self-discovery is an unsettling encounter where the self is seen as whole and hence produces both an alienation and abstraction with the flesh. The screen, as a historical artefact, represents a world beyond us. A world of dreams, hopes, fears and desires. A liminal space of affective coupling with other live forms represented through it. The appropriation of new media technologies into our everyday lives and its embedding onto our bodies meant we gained a renewed intimacy with the screen. The age of convergence facilitated us to insert ourselves into the screen, where we could be re-imagined as commodities, objects and subjects that could be transacted in the digital economy. The project of us watching ourselves is an elongation of the 'mirror moment' in the digital age where the mirror and screen become coalesced, invoking and reasserting our primal love for ourselves as a vital part of the digital economy. Capital stokes our love for ourselves in the digital age and constantly seduces us to partake in its enterprise under the guise of co-creation and the premise of empowerment offered through UGC. As such, the self in postmodernity is a vulnerable 'self', immersed in the invisible workings of capital. In postmodernity the screen becomes a mirror, where our sense of self is performed and enacted through a networked economy.

BIBLIOGRAPHY

Bahrick, Lorraine E. (1995). "Intermodal Origins of Self-Perception." In *The Self in Infancy: Theory and Research*, edited by P. Rochat, 349–373. Amsterdam: North-Holland-Elsevier Science.

Bahrick, Lorraine E., Moss, Lisa, & Faidl, Christine. (1996). "Development of Visual Self-Recognition in Infancy." *Ecological Psychology, 8*(3), 189–208.

Benjamin, Walter. (1995). *The Correspondence of Walter Benjamin, 1990–1940*. Translated by Manfred R. Jacobson and Evelyn M. Jacobson. Chicago: University of Chicago Press.

Bolter, David J., & Grusin, Richard A. (2000). *Remediation: Understanding New Media*. Boston, MA: MIT Press.

Bonsu, Samuel K., & Darmody, Aron. (2008). "Co-creating Second Life: Market-Consumer Cooperation in Contemporary Economy." *Journal of Macromarketing, 24*(4): 355–368.

Davies, Martin L. (1989). "History as Narcissism." *Journal of European Studies, 19*(4), 265–291.

Gibson, James J. (1950). *The Perception of the Visual World*. Boston: Houghton Mifflin.

Gibson, James J. (1986). *The Ecological Approach to Visual Perception*. Hillsdale, NJ: Lawrence Erlbaum Associates, Inc. (Original work published 1979).

Gallop, Jane. (1982) "Lacan's "Mirror Stage": Where to Begin." *SubStance, 11* (1982), 118–128.

Gibson, William. (1993). *Neuromancer*. London: Harper.

Heidegger, Martin. (1962). *Being and Time*. Translated by John Macquarrie & Edward Robinson. San Francisco: Harper Collins. (Original work published 1927).

Heidegger, M. (1972). *On Time and Being*. Translated by J. Stambaugh. New York: Harper and Row.

Heidegger, Martin. (1977). "The Question Concerning Technology." In *The Question Concerning Technology and Other Essays*, 3–33. New York: Garland Publishers.

Heeter, C. (1992). "Being There: The Subjective Experience of Presence." *Presence, Teleoperators, and Virtual Environments, 1*, 262–271.

Hogan, Bernie. (2010). "The Presentation of Self in the Age of Social Media: Distinguishing Performances and Exhibitions Online." *Bulletin of Science, Technology & Society, 30*(6), 377–386.

Ibrahim, Yasmin. (2015). "Instagramming Life: Banal Imaging and the Poetics of the Everyday." *Journal of Media Practice, 16*(1), 42–54.

Ibrahim, Yasmin. (2008a). "The New Risk Communities: Social Networking Sites and Risk." *International Journal of Media and Cultural Politics, 4*(2), 245–253.

Ibrahim, Yasmin. (2008b). "The Co-opted Body and Counter-Surveillance: The Body as Data and Surveillance." *International Journal of the Humanities, 5*(12), 1–8.

Ibrahim, Yasmin. (2009). "Social Networking Sites (SNS) and the 'Narcissistic Turn'." In *Collaborative Technologies and Applications for Interactive Information Design: Emerging Trends in User Experiences: Emerging Trends in User Experiences*, 82.

Ibrahim, Yasmin. (2011). "The Non-Stop "Capture": The Politics of Looking in Postmodernity." *The Poster, 1*(2), 167–185.

Ibrahim, Yasmin. (2012). "The Politics of Watching: Visuality and the New Media Economy." *International Journal of E-Politics (IJEP), 3*(1), 1–11.

Jameson, F. (1984). "Postmodernism, or the Cultural Logic of Late Capitalism." *New Left Review, 146*, 59–92.

Jameson, F. (1998). *The Cultural Turn: Selected Writings on the Postmodern, 1983–1998.* Verso: London.

Lacan, Jacques. (1998). *The Seminar Book XI: The Four Fundamental Concepts of Psychoanalysis.* Edited by Jacques-Alain Miller. Translated by Alan Sheridan. New York: W.W. Norton & Company.

Lacan, Jacques. (2006). *Ecrits.* New York: Norton.

McDougall, Joyce. (1986). *Theatres of the Mind: Illusion and Truth in the Psychoanalytic Stage.* London: Free Association Books.

Mahler, Margaret S., & Furer, Manuel. (1968). *On Human Symbiosis and the Vicissitudes of Individuation.* New York: International University Press.

Manovich, Lev. (2001). *The Language of New Media.* Boston, MA: MIT Press.

Merleau-Ponty, Maurice. (1964). "The Child's Relations with Others." In Maurice Meleau-Ponty (Ed.), *The Primacy of Perception*, 96–155. Translated by William Cobb. Evanston, Illinois: Northwestern University Press.

Minsky, Marvin. (1980). "Telepresence." *Omni*, June: 45–51.

Mulvey, Laura. (1975). "Visual Pleasure and Narrative Cinema." *Screen, 16* (3), 6–18.

Negroponte, Nicholas. (1995). *Being Digital.* New York: Alfred A. Knopf.

Papacharissi, Zizi. (2011). "Conclusion: A Networked Self." In *A Networked Society,* edited by Z. Papacharissi, pp. 304–318. New York: Routledge.

Pasek, Anne. (2014). "Seeing Yourself Strangely: Media Mirroring in Takehito Etani's The Third Eye Project." *Metaverse Creativity, 4*(2), 121–138.

Piaget, Jean. (1954). *The Construction of Reality in the Child.* New York: Basic Books.

Robinson, Laura. (2007). "The Cyberself: The Selfing Project Goes Online, Symbolic Interaction in the Digital Age." *New Media Society, 9,* 93–110

Rocamora, Agnès. (2011). "Personal Fashion Blogs: Screens and Mirrors in Digital Self-Portraits" *Fashion Theory, 15*(4), 407–424.

Rochat, Philippe, & Zahavi, Dan. (2011). "The Uncanny Mirror: A Re-framing of Mirror Self-Experience." *Consciousness and Cognition, 20*(2), 204–213.

Schoback, V. (1990). "Toward a Phenomenology of Cinematic and Electronic Presence: The Scene of the Screen." *Post Script: Essays in Film and the Humanities, 10*(1), 50–59.

Sheridan, Thomas B. (1992). "Musings on Telepresence and Virtual Presence." *Presence, Teleoperators, and Virtual Environments, 1,* 120–125.

Steuer, Jonathan. (1992). "Defining Virtual Reality: Dimensions in Determining Telepresence." *Journal of Communication, 42*(4), 73–93.

Terranova, Tiziana. (2000). "Free Labour: Producing Culture for the Digital Economy." *Social Text, 18* (2), 33–58.

Turkle, Sherry. (1995). *Life on the Screen: Identity in the Age of Internet.* New York: Simon & Schuster.

Turkle, Sherry. (2005). *The Second Self: Computers and the Human Spirit and Life on the Screen: Identity in the Age of the Internet.* London, UK: MIT Press.

Walker, Jill. (2005). "Mirrors and Shadows: The Digital Aestheticisation of Oneself." In *The Proceedings of Digital Arts and Culture,* 184–190.

Williams, Raymond. (1974). *Television: Technology and Cultural Form.* London, Fontana.

Yiu, Yvone. (2005). The Mirror and Painting in Early Renaissance Texts. *Early Science and Medicine, 10*(2), 187–210.

CHAPTER 2

Anchoring the Self Through the Banal, the Everyday and the Familiar

Abstract This chapter examines the production of the self through digital technologies and the domesticity of the everyday, in terms of its pace, rituals and familiarity. Photo- and video-sharing sites draw on everyday domesticity as a space for communion. The aestheticization of the self through its domesticity is therapeutic in enabling a connection with others and equally as a site of cultural production where the self is transacted and commodified. The consumption of the everyday through digital platforms and technologies whether it be food diaries, consumption patterns or everyday chores is important, as it draws on the familiar and perfunctory. The banal offers codes of communication that are instantly recognisable and resonant with distant strangers, but in also anchoring imaging technologies as 'tamed' through its domestication within the everyday. In an age of anxiety, the anchoring of the self through the everyday presents the 'self' as being intact and renewed through the familiar.[1]

Keywords Everyday • Imaging Technologies • Video Sharing Sites • Domesticity • Communion • Aestheticization • Rituals • Self-commodification

INTRODUCTION

This chapter examines the production of the self through digital technologies and the domesticity of the everyday, in terms of its pace, rituals and familiarity. Photo and video sharing sites draw on everyday domesticity as

© The Author(s) 2018
Y. Ibrahim, *Production of the 'Self' in the Digital Age*,
https://doi.org/10.1007/978-3-319-74436-0_2

19

a space for communion. The aestheticization of the self through its domesticity is therapeutic in enabling a connection with others and equally as a site of cultural production where the self is transacted and commodified. The consumption of the everyday through digital platforms and technologies whether it be food diaries, consumption patterns or everyday chores is important, as it draws on the familiar and perfunctory. The banal offers codes of communication that are instantly recognisable and resonant with distant strangers, but in also anchoring imaging technologies as 'tamed' through its domestication within the everyday. In an age of anxiety, the anchoring of the self through the everyday presents the 'self' as being intact and renewed through the familiar.

Just as physical spaces are places of gathering for those who belong and those who are displaced, the internet provides a convening space for disembodied presence. This is often viewed as a Manichean dualism between the occurrence of thought and material presence. Equally, this is seen as unleashing a virulent 'avatarism' (Donath 1998) that seeks to re-invent this virtual disembodiment by assuming different identities or by embracing a non-identity of anonymity. This cognitive engagement with the virtual sphere and the attendant consequences with regard to identity construction and re-invention has been an intrinsic aspect of digital technologies. Nevertheless the offline and online are not separate and compartmentalised entities. They are entwined in complex ways. In this complex coalescing of medium and matter, the self emerges as a hybridised entity between the virtual and the physical spaces.

Zygmunt Bauman (2000) theorised the home as a 'phantasmagoric' place—as electronic means of communication allow the radical intrusion of 'the realm of the far' into the 'realm of the near' through media such as the television. While television creates new possibilities for collapsing distant worlds into the home space, social media celebrates the intimate through the insertion of the self onto the screen. 'Autoscopic phenomena' refer to a heterogeneous class of re-duplications of one's own body and perceived self (Brugger 2002: 180). The autoscopic encounters of the self through digital technologies that coalesce with our everyday lives mean that the self is performed with and through the screen. These autoscopic encounters collapse space and place and equally the temporal and spatial offering the autoscopic self as both a performative commodity without relinquishing the immediacy or banality of the everyday as a scope for new forms of narratives and performances.

The notions of identity and the performative are tightly entwined in our digital lives. Our daily interactions and engagements online contribute to identity creation. As the banal and the perfunctory migrate to online spaces of communication, everyday life becomes performed online and these mediated rituals of communicating the mundane and ritualistic can be therapeutic while enabling the self to be consumed by others. Both the ways in which we perceive ourselves through our daily rituals and the ways in which others consume us are important to the notion of presence in digital culture. The communication of the daily rituals also inscribes a sense of place, demarcating certain spaces with a sense of familiarity and resonance online. As such the self is constantly produced and renewed through the everyday and now this may be enacted in user-generated content (UGC), particularly in video- and image-sharing sites. The diarisation of our lives and equally our exhibitionistic and performative qualities means the self is produced and consumed contemporaneously in online spaces as we go about our daily routines in our physical environments. Beyond the routine and perfunctory of the everyday, self-production online entails interaction with a wider world accessed through the screen and through our everyday interactions with others and media artefacts. For Henri Lefebvre (1991: 97), 'everyday life is profoundly related to activities, and encompasses them with all their differences and their conflicts; it is their meeting place, their bond, their common ground.' Mike Featherstone (1995) perceives the everyday as a site from which our conceptualisations, definitions and our life stories spring. It includes the routines, the taken for granted experiences, beliefs and practices. It is the ambit of the mundane and the ordinary but it also entails the reproduction and maintenance of life (Duncum 2002: 4).

Today, online video/image platforms such as YouTube, Photobucket, Flickr, Pinterest, Snapchat and Instagram are filled with the aestheticization of everyday practices. The banal and the routine have found new modes of exhibition and display in these sites. People's everyday experiences of what they eat, what they wear, grooming rituals or life hacks have ignited new attention economies that centre the banal and the routine. The insatiable curiosity about others and the desire for 'sneak peeks' into their lives has meant that the self has become an online commodity of transaction through its daily life interactions. The banal has an audience and it provides a means to form resonance with friends and strangers. As such, the banal and the everyday have found an interface with the digital. The virtual and the virtually beautiful become the quest in everyday life (Aguiar 2011: 5). João Valente Aguiar (2011) contends the aestheticization of everyday life coexists with the aestheticized production of the individual self. Here there is a transference of aesthetic properties to the centre of life where the usual and familiar emerge through new means of looking and experiencing the familiar and the mundane.

The notion of aesthetic here refers to not only distinctive and diverse objects of perception but also but to a distinctive mode of consciousness that grasps such objects to invoke sensory perceptions (Shusterman 2006: 1). Aesthetic experiences can be valuable and pleasurable and digital platforms and their appropriation into our everyday lives mark the expansion of our aesthetic fields where the self can be encoded onto the screen and consumed by the self and others. It invites new forms of sociality, sharing and participation. Paul Duncum points out that the complexity of modern life means that a fantasy life of play and desire lurks within it. Aesthetics matter in everyday life because through aesthetic practices people make individual and collective meaning (Gude 2008: 98). Terry Eagleton (1990) considers the relationship between artistic sensibilities and other cultural values, thereby broadening the subject of aesthetics to include its own uses and history. Today visual culture can be seen as a manifestation of aesthetics and a key site for the production of cultural meaning. Digital platforms filled with diarisation of the self and its everyday practices marks a moment of the mundane being a site of cultural values, pleasure, desires and exhibitionistic attributes where the screen transforms the banal into aesthetic conventions that can resonate with an audience eager to convene through the rituals of the everyday.

Hence the exhibition of the self through everyday practices and equally the appropriation of digital technologies into everyday life fuse new means of narrating and imaging the self through the gaze of others. Everyday life provides a platform that invites the gaze of others through the familiarity of everyday practices. Strangers looking into private zones reconstruct the everyday and banal as sites of new forms of fantasy, desire and ways to re-imagine the self reconstituted through the screen. Herman Bausinger (1984) contends that the everyday is characterised by what he called the 'inconspicuous omnipresence of the technical', where a range of technologies become naturalised to the point of becoming invisible yet mediating our sense of presence and reality. The project of self-construction online has entailed the sharing of our intimate and private moments with a perceived sense of audience eager to consume the self, crafted through its everyday experiences. We have as such made the representation of the everyday a vital content for consumption in online spaces (Ibrahim 2015a). The banal and routine is experienced both in the material world and equally through its projection, narration and exhibition online.

Engagement and consumption through the screen has experiential properties as the screen offers us a means to produce our disembodied selves that we can equally consume in real time while living out our daily lives for the gaze of others.

This duality is part of digital living where the corporeal experiences and lived experiences become conjoined. As bodies become domesticated through mobile technologies, life experiences become conjoined through the screen with the convergence of technologies and our ability to produce ourselves as content on the move while consuming the self as a commodified entity. The production of the self through the everyday is a necessary part of our sense of sociality and engagement with a community. But importantly it asserts the sense of presence in the digital environment by enacting the familiar and the perfunctory through the routines of the everyday. The digital age and our obsession with the self is also seen as a 'narcissistic turn' where we can produce and curate ourselves online (See Ibrahim 2009). This 'selfie' culture of relentlessly curating ourselves through our everyday and extraordinary experiences means the self is co-authored through the gaze of others, their endorsement, consumptions and comments in interactive platforms. As such the 'selfied' self is a vulnerable one where consumption and validation of others becomes a mechanism to access a presentational self where its values emerge through an external gaze.

The projection of the everyday onto the screen for sharing re-scripts the banal as content and an integral aspect of our aesthetics. This provides a re-narration for what we might take for granted in our everyday existence. While much has been written about the domestication of technology in our domestic environments, we need to reconsider how we have inscribed domesticity onto the screen as a means to communicate our presence on the screen and to equally live through the screen. Screen living has domesticated the banal and perfunctory as a form of resonant code of communication that engenders familiarity and solidarity with fellow humans in an age of anxiety and constant political disruptions. It forms the basis of not just presence but an essential element of sharing and sociality online. The sociality of the everyday by showcasing the intimate happenings of domesticity and the banal produces highly personal moments online and is part of our semantics of bonding with others in our everyday engagements online. This screen living assumes a degree of 'publicness' in enacting one's daily routines and in communicating the everyday. The constant thrusting of personal realms in public platforms then recasts the everyday into a performative mode where banal moments are 'performed' for the consumption of others. The aestheticization of everyday life is one of the most fundamental cultural dynamics of the past few decades (see Aguiar 2011). The re-enactment of our banal lives and the re-composing of our selves through digital platforms reflect the intimate ways in which technologies become part of self-production and curation, composing an external gaze as a mechanism to validate the self and its everyday existence. Foucault (1979: 100) refers to 'making one's life a work of art' and the digital platform and its interactive architecture unleashes new ways to re-make the everyday as content. Mike Featherstone (1996: vii) highlights the 'emphasis upon youth, fitness and beauty' where such aestheticization affords pleasure and becomes a guiding principle in the configuration of lifestyles. For Featherstone, the aestheticization of our everyday lives emphasises

> *immediacies, intensities, sensory overload, disorientation, the mêlée or liquefac-tion of signs and images, the mixing of codes, the unchained or floating signifiers of the postmodern depthless consumer culture where art and reality have switched places in an aesthetic hallucination of the real.* (Featherstone 1996: 24)

Aesthetics has without doubt moved into the core of our consumption and production rituals online. Hence the stylisation of everyday life cannot be reduced to transaction value alone (Skeggs 2004: 137) but needs to be appreciated through the experiential and resonant where connections can be made through its implicit codes of connectivity. The centrality of images anchor everyday experiences that re-fashion consumption as bound with the routine and lifestyle of others and their consumption experiences. The everyday, including everyday imagery, is especially important in creating our attitudes, knowledge and beliefs (Duncum 2002: 5) and importantly the notion of self. Everyday visual imagery can be influential in structuring thought, feelings and actions, precisely because they are so ordinary that they are so significant. Their ubiquity under-scores their importance (Duncum 2002: 5) and the implication of the self within these paradigms casts the self as re-produced through the everyday as a digital commodity for consumption.

The communication of the everyday, whether it be Snapchats of your breakfast or pet or sharing the aggravation of your delayed train, encode an implicit intimacy as these are resonant depictions of the everyday and the familiar of our social settings. The banal of the everyday renders a therapeutic element to digital communication. It underpins implicit codes of familiarity with which others can identify, re-inscribing a sense of domesticity to online spaces. The act of sharing asserts the reality of the encounter, validating it through the gaze of others. As such the 'banal of the everyday' stands in contrast with an attention economy where unexpected and salacious events punctuate our routine lives with breaking news of explosions and disruptions in an age of anxiety. Nevertheless, the production of the self is implicated in both these configurations. The aesthetics of the self then assumes a whole range of vernacular online where its everyday enactments constitute a mode of presenting the self through the screen and capturing its interface with the wider world. These everyday aesthetics captured through imagery saturate the fabric of everyday life and involve participation, sensuousness and desire (Featherstone 1991: 67). Everyday visual sites offer resources both for the realisation of desire and signs for the creation of identities.

The communication of the everyday, whether through text or images, has a transcendental value that converts life experiences into screen narratives in this 'age of anxiety' where we are constantly distracted by the next big event. The interplay of people's intimate and everyday routines communicated and consumed through a screen, which can equally call us to bear witness to other worlds and events beyond our control asserts the therapeutic value in consuming the familiar and inscribing the perfunctory of the everyday into social media platforms. The banal of the everyday has social value. As the 'non-event' of the banal saturates our image landscape with objects of domesticity, it lends an important role in asserting and sustaining normalcy and in enabling a communion with intimate and imagined audiences on social media platforms. Our notions of sociality are also constantly reconfigured through these public displays but equally in how others consume us. The reciprocity of offering our banal lives for others and an expectation that we are consumed through our daily routines becomes a means to pattern therapeutic communications online. The banal in the age of anxiety seeks to retain the routine, the patterns, and indeed the normalcy of our everyday lives as these become disrupted through unexpected events, which are constantly thrust into our lives without warning.

If the banal re-inserts the time and space of the everyday, the self is also constantly co-produced through a wider world of events and interactions beyond the banal of the everyday. The wider world of the political, popular culture, consumerism, national conversations and voyeurism of the digital world is what I term the 'fictive'. The fictive does not imply that the real is not encoded in the wider happenings of the world. The fictive here is defined as what is represented through a digital environment and landscape where we can gain proximity and intimacy that may not be afforded in the real world.

The fictive of the digital world allows the layperson to be part of wider political debates, to partake in world events and popular culture without being materially present in these events and happenings in offline spaces. This possibility to insert the self into a wide array of events, ranging from the popular to the political, is enabled through the interactivity and mobility of the internet where social conversations can signpost events and enable engagements with distant events both in terms of consumption of these online and the partaking of them through conversations and discussions. The convergence of technologies and the architecture of Web 2.0 presents the possibility to archive and curate images even when we don't produce or own them and as such to create an intimacy through our engagements and modes of consumption of the fictive. It presents us with unlimited possibilities to veer into virtual image galleries and video platforms and to curate images from a wide repertoire of offerings from professional to amateur productions. The immense digital landscape allows one to negotiate the sense of time and space and equally to re-position notions of intimacy and proximity with the wider world represented through the digital terrain. It allows us to tag, to like, to follow the stranger and the celebrity while showcasing these wider engagements through the projection of the self online. As such our imagination of the world is co-produced though these wider engagements while centring the self as an interlocutor between the fictive and the banal.

THE SCREEN SELF AND SELF-COMMODIFICATION

The passing of the terrestrial age into a digital one brought an immense and renewed awe with technology. The digital age, in contrast to the terrestrial age of broadcasting, is one that allows us to be inserted inside the screen. The age of broadcasting produced both a fascination with the screen and an ability to re-produce and project the world into our intimate social settings. It provided a means to represent a wider world and mediate it through a screen culture of consuming what was out there through the confines of the home. The screen domesticated through the hearth and home provided an intimacy to distant and remote world events

(Williams 1974). The screen over time acquired a social status of being a filter to the outside world. Unlike radio or print, the screen could fill one's senses with sights and sounds supplanting imagination while offering ways to consume the world. The screen, as a receptacle of popular culture, political events and a platform for marking national processions and sharing the traumatic, produced an incestuous bind over time, reifying it as a cultural and communal artefact that provided connections to the wider world through everyday consumption habits.

In the age of broadcasting, the domestication of the television and its centrality as a cultural artefact where it provided communion with an imagined community became underpinning factors that sustained the screen as a space of cultural veneration. The screen provided a means to gaze at others and to be mobile even in the private spaces of the home. The intimate relationship with television as a central technology in the home crafted the screen as an edifice for escape but equally for forms of sociality and in patterning our sense of time and space through broadcast schedules and the act of watching. The watching of television produced an imagined sense of solidarity with the unknown other. The screen produced this implicit social bond while asserting its dominance in the privacy of our homes. The screen as such was bound with domesticity and consumed through the pace and rhythm of domestic life. The screen prevailed as a filter for viewing another world, signifying a place of make-believe and escape. The screen's association with make-believe and its ability to showcase the powerful and the deviant, or celebrity, or the suffering of the unknown expanded our field of vision beyond the immediate surrounds to encompass another world of staging events and productions. The screen provided the technical orifice for entering another world and hence the screen symbolised not just the expansion of vision and our ability to see beyond our immediate surroundings but also the possibility of immersing ourselves into alternate realities far removed from our own. The screen acquired a prominence in modernity where it was the source of entertainment, information and mass communication in society. This doubling of our field of vision through the screen made it an intimate part of reality construction in modernity.

The emergence of various forms of mobile gadgets again valorised the screen but also introduced the possibilities for solitary pleasure. The advent of the internet age and the incorporation of PCs and laptops in work environments as well as the home enabled us to think about the screen as a place where we could control, produce and mediate content directly. We could capture ourselves and others through the convergence of technologies and through mobile gadgets. It enabled an obsession to image ourselves and others non-stop and in the process it produced different forms of gaze enabled through existing power relationships as well as through the subversion of prevailing norms (See Ibrahim 2011).

The screen became much more malleable beyond watching one's favourite movies through the video recorder or the DVD. With the World Wide Web and the possibilities to browse disparate content, to communicate synchronously and asynchronously, the screen transcended into a much more personal artifice truncating it from its earlier social role as the immobile centrepiece in the living room. As the screen became more personalised through PCs and laptops, it came to signify much more intimate and private engagements while mediating a wider world through it. With the convergence of technologies, the advent of Web 2.0, increased bandwidth, along with the refinements in hand-held smart technologies, which targeted the corporeal body rather than the physical space of the home, the screen entered a new era of social relevance. The body as a site for embedding smart communication technologies produced the self as constantly mediated through both its physical space and the virtual one enabled through the screen. If the screen acquired social resonance and dominance in the age of broadcasting, it acquired a bodily intimacy in the age of the digital media, becoming an extension of the body where it was possible to ubiquitously consume the world as well as our selves online while simultaneously offering ourselves to others for consumption.

Beyond the 'intimatisation' of the screen, the transcendence from the broadcasting age to the social media age was marked through our ability to see ourselves inside the screen. The screen no longer belonged to the powerful or the celebrity, it became a space in which one could view oneself and offer the self to others as an object and subject. The self became part of content production online and became a means to fill the spaces of social media platforms, becoming part content and part data where these can be transacted with and without human consent. The inserting of the self onto screens, our ability to consume and narrate ourselves and equally to make ourselves content for the consumption of friends and strangers extended the social importance of the screen in the digital age. The screen belonged to us and we started to belong to the screen.

With reality television, the loss of scripting and the demise of production values were critiqued. Nevertheless, reality television made confessional television and the consumption of ordinary people part of the fabric of television. The changing political economy of broadcasting, particularly the shift from terrestrial to satellite and cable, banished issues with spectrum scarcity and enabled a whole array of niche lifestyle and reality programmes to saturate television. It led to criticisms about the loss of quality and the demise of the public sphere and public service broadcasting, with less funding routed to public information and education programmes. The incorporation of reality television and the re-fashioning of the public gaze to view the ordinary and intimate details of people's everyday lives became a precursor in enabling the perfunctory and the everyday to become part of media content. The unscripted watching of people and leveraging on people performing for the camera or 'acting up' constituted a new era of watching others but equally envisioned the screen as part of the exposure. Equally it re-inscribed the banal and domestic routines of people's uneventful lives and the ordinariness of existence to become viable subjects. Television, veering beyond the valued principles of education, information and communication, entered a phase of perverse and pervasive people watching, which the digital age sought to expand infinitum. However it went a step further where people could watch themselves and also offer themselves for others to watch. Self-gaze became an intrinsic component of watching in the digital era and hence it created the aestheticization of the self, evident in the rise and rise of selfies and a whole repository of advice and technical proficiency in presenting and curating the self aesthetically online.

With social media, the self became commodified as content and data—as a commodity for exchange and transaction. It provided a means for people to insert themselves onto the screen. This self-commodification again reconfigured the relationship with the screen and equally the narration of the routine and banal as content online. Prior to the digital age we domesticated technologies such as the television and other domestic appliances into our private realm. In the digital age the technologically embodied body co-opted the banal and the routine in our private domains as content for social media and new media platforms. The corporeal embedding of technology meant it entered a much more intimate realm than that of the age of television. While television as a technology projected content from outside, the technologically embodied self projected the domestic and banal, or what may been deemed as private, onto the outer world. Technology's conquest of the body also meant an increasing loss of inhibition and increasing blurring of boundaries on what can be deemed public or private. As technologies became part of the body and extended vision, memory and sensory perceptions let us live our lives through the screen, the banal and the everyday became genres of content in which others could find communion and resonance. The digital age in essence made the banal an intrinsic part of sociality and in gaining intimacy with others.

While mobile gadgets privatised the screen by decoupling it from the domestic environment, social media inverted the screen into a mirror where people could watch themselves forging an intense intimacy through the everyday and in terms of transforming the self into a disembodied entity online. The screen was no longer just a private or solitary space but one that recorded 'the daily and the everyday' and projected it to others updating on the movements and experiences of the self.

While reality television enabled us to insert ordinary people onto the screen and consume them, social media enabled the self to be part of the content of the screen enabling visibility to a wider audience and propelling the self into a public arena. This duality of the self where life is experienced through one's physical environment and, equally, through how it is experienced and narrated online means that the screen acquired a projective quality of extending the real into the virtual. The public quality of social media platforms enabled the self to become a performative entity and to exist through the consumption and the endorsement of an imagined public.

With the proliferation of new channels and programmes through cable and satellite broadcasting, social media conceived the hoi polloi as content. While imparting notions of its democratic potential as a people's communication tool, social media leveraged on people as content and data to drive these platforms and to create value (see Bonsu and Darmody 2008; Terranova 2000). It extracted people and their daily lives as content. The digital platforms enticed people to share stories, direct gaze, to endorse people, products and services, and to signpost information, but most importantly to sign up to an economy where these creative enterprises, whether in the form of text, videos or images, did not foreclose people revealing the personal and the intimate and courting public gaze. While the empowering qualities of the internet and social media platforms were constructed through issues of access, connectivity and the ability to transform people into public entities, they laid claims to the commodification of the self and creating value through the public transaction of the self. It in many ways symbolised the ultimate triumph of capitalism where the self could be monetised and transacted as content and data in online platforms while creating value for advertisers and social media sites by joining them to products and services. The lure of the screen and our awe with it also meant the increasing loss of inhibition where we are willing to be intimate and public on the screen. The monetisation of the self meant that we as digital tribes became complicit in the digital economy of exchange and value creation. Equally, we became complicit in wanting to share our lives online and hence became part of the complicit risk economy (Ibrahim 2008a).

As social media commodified the self, it also became a place to share the banal and the perfunctory aspects of everyday life. Social media eager to fill empty spaces on digital platforms, offered the self as a commodity for transaction and consumption in a mediated world. The domesticity of the everyday, our everyday routines and the perfunctory became means to narrate our lives and to offer them as content for others to consume. In the process we consumed ourselves and also sought to see how others consumed us through page visits and endorsements such as likes, reposting and re-tweeting. The ubiquity of mobile technologies, their co-location on the corporeal body and the emergence of a sociality through the everyday made the banal a resonant part of human communication and communion.

'JE SUI WORLD'

The participatory elements in new media technologies, the ability to partake in public conversations and the democratic potential to be a producer of content online, enabled the self to be narrated beyond the banal or the perfunctory. The self and its engagement with the world and the public nature of these engagements sought to narrate the self through wider events of the world and the market place. The self, through its Instagram or Twitter accounts, could be part of the conversation and as such it was re-fashioned from purely narcissistic production modes to those in which it interacted with world events. The self as a reactive and expressive entity to the wider world composed through the screen is also an important part of identity creation today. Thus beyond our composition through the everyday, the wider world and its happenings co-construct the self. While broadcasting sought to reconfigure our notions of space and time through the screen, the social media age intensified this. By mediating the virtual world through the screen, time and space are not only reconfigured but a distinct proximity is created through our engagements with the fictive world as represented on the screen. The convergence of technologies means that we not only gaze but consume and communicate ubiquitously and we expect an instant gratification from our activities online, afforded through synchronous communication such as chat facilities and people reading posts in real time and endorsing these.

In contrast to the broadcast age, the screen does not only double the vision into an alternate reality but also enables the self to be re-cast with world events through the ability to partake in them through discussions, signposting, re-tweeting, blogs, image curation, and so forth. The self can express solidarity with renunciations of atrocities or commune with trauma where these occur. The self has become a means to stand in solidarity and to co-produce it as a symbol of protest during times of crisis. The rise of 'solidarity selfies' reveals the entity of the self as an active agent in terms of political engagement. The re-fashioning of the self as part of another person's trauma or misfortune not only communicated the solidarity in these enactments but equally the potency of employing the self as a political tool to express disaffection, citizenship, protest or communion with the dispossessed. The rise of solidarity selfies doesn't necessarily decentre the self but provides a means to locate politics through its disembodied representation online while using it as a form of political expression. In numerous political contexts and situations of social dissent, the selfie has become a hybrid form of social protest, of standing in consensus with the crowd yet employing the individual self to be part of the collective. Hence the 'fictive' of the wider world becomes renegotiated through the sense of self online both through its political orientations and the self as an entity for public and symbolic protest. The new media screen allows the individual to delve into the virtual and to be mobile within its offering and to exercise choice and agency. While television was about mobile privatisation, new media allowed one to go beyond and to add to the content creation online. Thus images could be re-hashed and real events can be satirised through memes and mashups. Real-world events can be narrated through UGC and personal commentary to re-configure the sacred and puerile in the virtual world. People can elongate event creation by partaking in both celebrations and tragedies online through the projection of the self onto the screen. As such digital platforms have become spaces to enact new rituals of mourning and celebration and to create social norms where the self is never completely decentred.

If television allowed us to witness tragedies and be part of national mourning and celebration through the notion of mass audience and consumption, the mobile screen of tablets and smartphones personalised our engagements with the wider world. It allowed us to be selective with what we let onto our screens while being enticed into a whole array of content online through cookies and algorithms that track preferences and seek attention constantly. Watching communally also entails the phenomenon of 'second screening' where people interact with content while they consume it. It conjoins a connection with a wider audience where it was previously imagined through the nation state in the age of broadcasting (see Anderson 1991). If the age of broadcasting prior to the notion of 'television on demand' sought to order time and space through broadcasting schedules and to impose the notion of an imagined community through broadcasting in a nation state, the personal screen of today has made it a reality for us to speak to this 'imagined' community while consuming, watching and relating our comments in real time. Our public spheres forming through text and images are exchanged in real time.

The digital age is an age of distraction, where advertising content and alerts add layers to the screen vision, seeking to distract and divert the self elsewhere. While the screen of mass consumption as conceived through television sought to deliver a mass-mediated world, the small screen signified by the personalised gadget fractured and personalised the virtual arena, seeking to impress the self as an individual with its own preferences and agency. While the proliferation of multiple channels on the television screen stood for choice and leisure, the small screen of fracture is a screen that conjoins several platforms including television programmes and UGC. It stands for a distraction economy where the engagement of the self in terms of content can leave a data trail while creating a browser history unique to it (Ibrahim 2008b). Hence the self is constantly narrated through its data trail where it can be coded as part of big data and equally through its unique preferences and settings. If the screen stood for communion in the age of broadcasting, in the digital age the screen is a fluid space that requires the self to be both performed and coded through its consumption and preferences. The digital screen requires a more active engagement, seeking to build private spaces through logins and passwords while seeking to render one a subject of wider invisible processes of turning everything into data.

CARNAL DESIRE AND THE SELF

Deep within the intimate settings of the everyday, the self is in constant entanglement with various forms of desire where the corporeal body becomes an object of external gaze and equally bodily desires can be played out through the screen. One increasing realm of fantasy creation is that of food production and consumption. Food imagery as a form of transacted materiality online offers familiarity, comfort, co-presence but above all a common elemental literacy where food transcends cultural barriers, offering a universal pull towards a commodity that is ephemeral yet preserved through the click economy (Ibrahim 2015b). One such phenomenon is the *Mukbang* (or *Meokbang* in Korean). In literal terms it is an eating show in which the host eats vast amounts of food while interacting with the audience. Here the self enters a journey of carnal desire with others through the consumption of food. While increasing governance of the body in modernity entailed the strict regulation of food through scientific and medical knowledge that warn against excess and setting limits on dietary intake, the *Mukbang* in contrast is the virtual acting out of the bodily sins of gluttony where desire for insatiable amounts of food and the pornographic gaze of audience rests not on control and governance of the body but its excess. These videographies of food signify the celebration of desire and excess and equally the re-fashioning of the self as something that is in sustained interplay with desire and its limits online. The corporeal body is constantly re-fashioned through its virtual manifestation online. The excess of 'food porn' and its intimate trysts with one of the seven original sins project the self to new forms of visuality online. The act of others watching the physical consumption of food, on digital platforms, inserts the notions of desire, excess, social deviance and re-mediation of bodily pleasures as a vital yet subliminal part of cultural production in the online environment. Banal acts of food consumption and production seek to thwart and resist the extreme regulation of the body and its dietary intake in modernity where excess food consumption induces guilt and shame. The pleasures of watching the excesses of others project one's own forbidden desires as a site of pleasure online. The banal is a space to re-imagine life's routines and equally the re-mediation of guilt and shame induced through excessive regulation of the body and its bodily image in modernity.

CONCLUSION

The notions of the banal and the fictive provide a means to interrogate how the self is performed through the everyday and through world events where these provide a theatre to narrate the self and its engagements. The banal is part of self-objectification where our ability to insert ourselves onto the screen enables us to perform the self through everyday routines and rituals. This exposition of the banal is a therapeutic element of communion and sociality today. The objectification of the self also devises a more intense relationship with the screen where notions of privacy and intimacy and of being connected became re-configured. The intense relationship with the screen and the transformation of the self as an object of consumption through its daily rituals provide a means to fill a vast abyss of digital terrain with content. The self is both content and data online where it is both consumed and transacted through algorithms, creating value for advertisers and organisations. In contrast to the banal, the self is also narrated through a wider world of events where the self is imagined by inserting it into trauma, celebrations, and rituals of mourning and protest. The engagement with the fictive allows the self to be more than just a voyeur in the new media economy. It can partake and elongate event creation without decentring the self while sustaining itself as a form of commodity for others to consume. The fictive of the wider world can be owned, curated and co-produced through the self in this digital screen culture.

NOTE

1. An earlier version of this chapter appeared as Ibrahim, Y. (2016). Self-Production through the Banal and the Fictive: Self and the Relationship with the Screen. *International Journal of E-Politics*, 7(2), 51–61.

BIBLIOGRAPHY

Aguiar, J.V. (2011). "The Aestheticization of Everyday Life and the De-classicization of Western Working-Classes." *The Sociological Review*, 59(3), 616–632.

Anderson, B. (1991). *Imagined Communities: Reflections on the Origins and Spread of Nationalism*. London: Verson.

Bauman, Z. (2000). *Liquid Modernity*. Cambridge: Polity.

Bausinger, H. (1984). "Media, Technology and Daily Life." *Media Culture & Society*, 6(4), 343–351.

Bausinger, Herman. "Media, Technology and Everyday Life." *Media, Culture and Society*, 6(4), 343–352.

Bonsu, Samuel K., & Darmody, Aron. (2008). "Co-creating Second Life: Market-Consumer Cooperation in Contemporary Economy." *Journal of Macromarketing*, 24(4), 355–368.

Brugger, P. (2002). "Reflective Mirrors: Perspective-Taking in Autoscopic Phenomena." *Cognitive Neuropsychiatry*, 7(3), 179–194.

Donath, J.S. (1998). "Identity and Deception in the Virtual Community." In *Communities in Cyberspace*, edited by M.A. Smith and P. Kollock. New York: Routledge.

Duncum, P. (2002). "Clarifying Visual Culture Art Education." *Art Education*, 55(3), 6–11.

Eagleton, T. (1990). *The Ideology of the Aesthetic*. Maiden, MA: Blackwell Publishers.

Lefebvre, H. (1991). *Critique of Everyday Life*. Translated by John Moore. London: Verso.

Gude, O. (2008). "Aesthetics Making Meaning." *Studies in Art Education*, 50(1), 98–103. Retrieved from http://www.jstor.org/stable/25475889

Featherstone, M. (1991). *Consumer Culture and Post Modernism*. London: Sage.

Featherstone, M. (1995). *Undoing Culture: Globalization, Postmodernism and Identity*. London: Sage.

Featherstone, M. (1996). *Consumer Culture and Postmodernism*. London: Sage.

Foucault, M. (1979). *The History of Sexuality: Volume One, an Introduction*. London: Penguin.

Ibrahim, Y. (2015a). "Instagramming Life: Banal Imaging and the Poetics of the Everyday." *Journal of Media Practice*, 16(1), 42–54.

Ibrahim, Y. (2015b). "Food Porn and the Invitation to Gaze: Ephemeral Consumption and the Digital Spectacle." *International Journal of E-Politics*, 6(3), 1–12.

Ibrahim, Yasmin. (2008a). "The New Risk Communities: Social Networking Sites and Risk." *International Journal of Media and Cultural Politics*, 4(2), 245–253.

Ibrahim, Yasmin. (2008b). "The Co-opted Body and Counter-Surveillance: The Body as Data and Surveillance." *International Journal of the Humanities*, 5(12), 1–8.

Ibrahim, Yasmin. (2009). "Social Networking Sites (SNS) and the 'Narcissistic Turn'." In *Collaborative Technologies and Applications for Interactive Information Design: Emerging Trends in User Experiences: Emerging Trends in User Experiences*, 82.

Ibrahim, Yasmin. (2011). "The Non-Stop "Capture": The Politics of Looking in Postmodernity." *The Poster*, 1(2), 167–185.

Ibrahim, Yasmin. (2012). "The Politics of Watching: Visuality and the New Media Economy." *International Journal of E-Politics (IJEP)*, 3(1), 1–11.

Shusterman, R. (2006). "Aesthetic Experience: From Analysis to Eros." *The Journal of Aesthetics and Art Criticism*, 64(2), 217–229.

Skeggs, B. (2004). *Class, Self, Culture*. London and New York: Routledge

Terranova, T. (2000). "Free Labour: Producing Culture for the Digital Economy." *Social Text 18*(2), 33–58.

Williams, R. (1974). *Television: Technology and Cultural Form*. London: Fontana.

CHAPTER 3

Self-Love and Self-Curation Online

Abstract The self is constantly curated through an image-laden economy from the narcissistic turn to 'lifecasting' online. This chapter examines the notion of self-love and how our image-saturated worlds induce new modes of sociality that centre the transaction and curation of the self online. The coalescing of the mirror and screen produce a new-found fascination with a self which is aestheticized and constantly curated for others but most importantly validated through this gaze. This notion explores the concept of glass-house society where the act of watching defines new modes of self-curation and sociality.

Keywords Self-love • Self-curation • Self-objectification
• Self-asetheticization • Imaging technologies • Banal imaging
• Narcissism • Self-exposure

INTRODUCTION

This chapter examines the curation of the self through social networking sites and how these have mediated the emergence of a profile economy online. This creates a form of spectacular 'glass-house' society where the act of 'watching the self being consumed by others' creates an economy where the gaze of others becomes relevant and political in the formation of an online self. This induces news forms of sociality and performativity where our public enactments have a ubiquitous interface with a larger

© The Author(s) 2018   37
Y. Ibrahim, *Production of the 'Self' in the Digital Age*,
https://doi.org/10.1007/978-3-319-74436-0_3

public composed of friends and strangers. This chapter examines the notion of self-love or amour-proper by reviewing how the self is commodified through the online platform and how it performs to the notion of desire—its own and that of others.

According to Greek mythology, when Narcissus saw his reflection in a pond he fell in love with his own image; he was so consumed with this self-image that he stopped eating and eventually died. This myth suggests that seeing oneself through the perspective of others can be unsettling, raising the difficult issue of self-love and presenting oneself as a commodity or a source of desire to others and oneself. The screen self on our domesticated screen is a problematic encounter that raises questions about our relationship with this manifest self online. Martin Davies (1989: 265) asserts for European culture the Narcissus myth is subversive as it reflects 'self-knowledge' as the outcome of a strange madness to know oneself, which ultimately results in the agony of death. The myth is also about Western subjectivity where the quest for uniqueness or particularity is an arrogant obsession that can be ultimately self-destructive.

Banal imaging can be situated under the ambit of personal photography, which has been the subject of research in many fields including sociology, anthropology and visual studies (Barthes 1981; Chalfen 1987; Bourdieu 1990; Rose 2003). More specifically, it is anchored in the sociology of the everyday, where the recording of the mundane and routine through imagery turns it into the performative. Life's rich and trivial moments are commodified so they can be transacted and shared, inviting new forms of gaze while enabling the everyday to be aestheticized and the self to be inserted in these compositions. Those images are then consumed by the self and others who have an implicit understanding of these conventions of the everyday. These banal images become part of self-representation and are bound to a social-media economy in which digital presence entails creating personal content, commodifying it and sharing it. This social media economy therefore hinges on the primacy of the image.

With increasing incorporation of mobile technologies with high-resolution image capture facilities, Wi-Fi connectivity as well as increased data storage functions (including cloud computing), the age of convergence crafts the corporeal body as a site of technological habitation, where the physiological and cognitive abilities to watch, consume and remember images become somewhat elongated through technology. Wearable technology then extends the sensory functions of the body, blurring the boundaries between the corporeal body and technology. This mobile body embedded with technology extends the ability to freeze frame images in real time, and to disseminate, archive and retrieve these on digital platforms. The ubiquity of the mobile phone well as the rise of smartphones has enabled image capture and storage on a large scale, unleashing a wider digital visual culture where images are shared, exchanged and commodified on video/image sharing sites and apps. The aestheticization of the mundane and trivial in our everyday lives calls into focus the ways in which communication in the Web 2.0 economy appropriates a visual bias where semantic communication is also augmented by the symbolic. Our domestication of media technologies and the extension of these onto the corporeal body patterns communication through our everyday engagement with the wider world through mobile technologies. The leap of media technologies from a domestic setting to the corporeal body makes technology intimate with our movements, pace of life, sensorial and aesthetic senses.

The 'curatorial turn' in the formation of the self in the digital platform is facilitated by increased interactivity and video/image uploading capacities, and improved broadband and bandwidth along with enhanced camera functions on mobile phones. Digital imaging through digital devices does not incur processing costs and transcends tangible material reproduction to be seamlessly published and shared on digital and mobile platforms. It can be commodified without a manifest tangibility to its format or circulation. It draws on the sociological concept of the 'everyday', where the patterns and routines of the private realm may become public (Harrison 2002). Harrison points out that private images have a transcendental role in negotiating private and public realms. Personal photography, particularly the commodification of the self, threatens the boundaries between the public and private.

The autoscopic possibilities of new media signal an unsettling moment for humanity. The notion of presence is then concerned with the subjective feeling of existence within a given environment (Heeter 1992). Early discourses of the internet celebrated not only the ability to re-invent identity online but also the concept of 'avatarism' where a user can have multiple identities. But although this can certainly be empowering it can also enable new forms of deception. New forms of narcissism enabled by social networking sites (SNSs), however, celebrate the notion of constructing one's offline profile online and inviting others to start friendships through such representations of self. Early discourses of the internet and present debates about the World Wide Web indicate that identity is a contentious and fragmented construct in view of the absence of physical cues in a discursive and, subsequently, a multimedia environment (Stefanone et al. 2008: 107). Compared to the earlier internet environment, which leveraged on experimentation with identity, today's computer-mediated communication aligns the users closer to their offline selves. The increasing emphasis on existing offline identities and relationships, physical and non-verbal communication cues and manipulation defines the nature of computer-mediated communication today (Stefanone et al. 2008). As the digital platform provides the mirror and screen experiences to resurrect the self as a commodity for consumption by the self and others, the self is a source of new forms of desire and gaze. The desire to curate a digital self, which is immersed in and acknowledged through the gaze and validation of others, invariably crafts an age of anxiety where we are vulnerable and sensitive to this consumption economy.

SELF IN THE AGE OF SOCIAL NETWORKING SITES

Unlike earlier websites, which thrived on the notion of anonymity and virtuality, social media emphasises the declaration of real offline identities to participate in the networking phenomenon. While the forerunners of SNSs in the 1990s included sites such as Classmates.com, the advent of the new millennium heralded a new generation of websites that celebrated the creation of self-profiles. Friendster, for example, attracted over 5 million registered users in a span of a few months in 2002 (see Rosen 2007). Friendster was soon followed by MySpace, Livejournal.com and Facebook, and these sites convened around existing offline communities such as college students. In the case of MySpace the site was originally launched by musicians to upload and share videos while Facebook initially catered to college students but is presently open to anyone who wants to network socially online. Some of these sites have witnessed phenomenal growth since their inception.

The creation and exhibition of self-profiles can be historically located and is not unique to the new-media environment. Christine Rosen (2007) points out that historically the rich and powerful documented their existence and status through painted portraits. In contemporary culture using a SNS is akin to having one's portrait painted, although the comparative costs make SNSs much more egalitarian. She contends that these digital 'self-portraits' signify both the need to re-create identity through the online platform as well as to form social connections. For Rosen (2007: 15), the resonant strand that emerges is the 'timeless human desire for attention'.

With SNSs there is a shift in the re-making of identity. While social connective sites in the 1990s illuminated the sense of place with home pages, global villages and cities, with SNSs there has been an emphasis on the creation of the 'self' through a multitude of interactions. According to Boyd and Heer (2006: 2), 'the performance of social identity and relationships through profiles has shifted these from being a static representation of self to a communicative body in conversation with other represented bodies. The emphasis of self-expression through the creation of profiles then anchors publicity, play and performance at the core of identity formation and communication.' As such identity is mutable, online and not embodied by the body, often the need to disclose real-life identities is intimately tied to this community's code of authenticity in making identity claims where friends and peers can verify claims made in the profiles (Donath and Boyd 2004).

A multitude of phenomena online has renewed interest in the notion of self-love. Digital culture mediated through interactive platforms today lays renewed emphasis on self-representation and self-construction. This has been alluded to as the 'narcissistic turn' (Ibrahim 2009) where new media had, prior to this, celebrated the notion of anonymity and disembodied presence divorced from our offline selves. This online avatarism was seen as heralding a new form of emancipation where we could discard and re-invent identities and indeed not declare our real selves to others. With the emergence of social media, particularly SNSs, and increasing capitalisation on profile building and profile sharing as forms of social capital, the self is again at the forefront of identity construction. It is part of a wider consumption and exchange economy, in which the gaze of others has an important bearing on how we perceive ourselves in this digital culture. Rather than viewing this as a purely narcissistic turn and hence as a negative manifestation of human behaviour, the renewed interest in the construction and presentation of the self online and validation by others needs a review of its therapeutic elements and the ethics of constructing ourselves through the gaze and endorsement of others in our contemporary digital culture.

It would be too reductionist to frame self-love as a purely negative phenomenon that gives rise to extreme emotions of envy and jealousy detrimental to not just one's self-development but also that of a community. In effect, a better understanding of self-love online can shed light on human frailties and equally how the politics of identity creation online are intricately entwined with how we are watched and rated by others. It is important to underline here that the gaze of others watching us has intrinsic power, for it can shape and influence the ways in which we construct our own identities and our perceptions of ourselves in the community. This act of 'watching others watch us' leads to wider questions about our dependence on others rating us, tagging us, following us or liking us. The social capital we create online is one that is inimically bound to a peer community of onlookers (and strangers) and their gaze. This brings forth new forms of vulnerabilities created through this comparative gaze.

It is well accepted today that profile building on SNSs plays a significant role in identity creation, where the sense of self is shaped through peer validation and gaze. In line with this, it is important to understand the online economy as one of public spectacle. This 'spectacular economy' unleashes a pervasive gaze where we constantly watch others and equally are aware of others watching us. We cease to be neutral entities online. Beyond our own agency to represent ourselves, the online economy of consumption, reciprocity and gaze plays a significant role in ascribing a social value to our presence and profile. The complex politics of self-identity online is both bound to our self-love and equally how others rate us. In tandem with this, a whole host of behaviours have emerged online to represent the self and equally to seek the validation of others through technical features that allow us to show endorsement of others and equally express censure or vitriol. Self-love and public validation and the construction of public identity are then bound in intricate ways online in this digital economy.

Online and offline identities are bound in complex ways and are not dichotomised. As mentioned, social media today emphasises a representational identity visible and manifested through multimedia platforms. Beyond the avatarism discourses of re-inventing identities online, social-media identity formed through peer communities is enmeshed with our offline identity. The distinctive element of our online identity is that it relies on public consumption and validation of the self through others.

The Self and the 'Spectacular' Online Economy

Social media sociality brings numerous ethical and moral challenges for humanity in living our lives publicly and in seeking validation through a peer economy, and as such it re-asserts the salience of the concept of amour-propre or 'self-love' in digital culture. Today we can perform identities online and indeed the politics of identity formation online are mediated both by technology, social norms, culture and our psychological states. What we do recognise is that self-presentation and identity are intimately implicated in online digital cultures. The online environment presents possibilities for the 'curation' of self and to be engaged with peer communities online. Self-representation can happen through our communication rituals online and our interaction with others. The notion of self can be entwined with networks, particularly SNSs, which are embedded with everyday communication and sharing of ourselves, encompassing the trivial, the everyday and the eventful moments with others. As such the concept of 'amour-propre' or self-love acquires a renewed relevance in the digital economy through its attendant sociability, where we can perform our identities, become part of a collective and yet stand out through our unique presence online whether through our profile or through our interactions online.

Today, an integral aspect of the curation of the self is also bound up with the notion of desire for oneself and equally how we may be commodified for others. Mimetic desires in society underscore the deeply social and cultural character of desire, where consumer desire can be an affirmation of belonging in a globalising consumer culture (Belk 2003: 347) and equally niche communities offline and online. Consumption and mimetic desires become a source of inspiration, transcendence and even redemption where desire re-iterates the sense of being alive and in some sense to hold back death (O'Shea 2002). As such, desire breaks the monotony of routine. Belk (2003) in reviewing desire as a concept points out that the vitality and pleasure of desire rest on breaking the order, monotony, routines, limits, and rules, but on the other hand, self-control, moral conduct, sociality and mimesis are themselves desirable. These tensions are neither solely between the individual's desires and social or self-constraints nor only between desires and sin. The tension is also between the individual's own social, affective, moral desires (as in the desire for sociability) and more transgressive desires. This is an internal personal struggle with a social basis, echoing Bataille's (1967) idea about interdictions and their transgression as constitutive of sociality and individuality. In the digital environment these tensions are played out in constituting the self. The self located through extreme consumerism, and as a transacted commodity online presents itself through new forms of desires—its own and those of others.

Foucault in *The Care of the Self* (1986: 42) articulates that individualism involves an attitude of independence towards a group of people, a valuation of private life and 'an intensity of the relations to self, that is, of the forms in which one is called upon to take oneself as an object of knowledge and a field of action, so as to transform, correct, and purify oneself, and find salvation'. Rosi Braidotti argues that the 'construction of a thinking subject cannot be separated from that of a desiring subject' reminds us that 'desire is the first and foremost step in the process of constitution of a self' (2002: 71).

Modern subjects appear to engage in self-monitoring to assure that they do not seem foolish but also to assure that they do not seem backward and dead to the world (Belk 2003: 348). Not being dead then details a production of presence online where the self is constructed through its agency and activities. With digital culture we have a palpable sense of others constantly watching and rating us. Today ego-surfing and self-googling is a socially resonant phenomenon where millions of people vanity search, making it a major online activity (McNicol 2009). A Pew survey conducted in April and May of 2013 showed that 56% of internet users in the USA had used a search engine to look up their own name to ascertain what information is available about them online, this constituted a 22% rise in vanity searching compared to 2001 (Madden 2013). As with many reputation-related activities online, adults under the age of 50 are more likely than older adults to monitor their digital footprints. And those with higher levels of education and household income (who tend to have jobs that require online reputation monitoring) are among the most likely to self-search (Madden 2013). Similarly a study of people's motives for using, and uses of, Facebook reveals that people use it for two main reasons: to monitor what contacts and friends are doing and as a self-presentation tool (Joinson 2008).

The new economy lends to the 'performative and exhibitionistic' where the self is constantly curated. While Rousseau spoke of the village festivals as a means to showcase talent and reveal one's distinctiveness, the digital economy affords the publicness where a collective gaze can fall and where the self can be performed, inviting validation or censure from others. The need to attract public attention in some way through daily interactions and to seek familiar and unknown audiences characterises SNSs. Stefanone et al. (2008) maintain that this behaviour is linked to the 'celebrity culture' that is evident in mainstream media and particularly in television genres such as reality TV. With user-generated content (UGC) and the ability to host profiles on interactive sites the Web 2.0 environment enables users to participate in celebrity culture by constructing themselves as active personas online.

Stefanone et al. (2008: 107) contend that new multimedia technologies erode 'the behavioural and normative distinctions between the celebrity world and the mundane everyday lives of the users'. They argue that the dissolution of this boundary is discernible in two resonant strands: the popularisation of the reality television genre and the proliferation of SNSs that hinge on the revelation of offline identities. They identify these two trends as reconfiguring the media environment where audiences are more than the recipients of media messages. Audiences as users and consumers can become 'protagonists of media narratives and can integrate themselves into a complex media ecosystem' (Stefanone et al. 2008: 107). They argue that platforms such as SNSs emphasise aspects of human interaction that have been traditionally associated with celebrity including the primacy of image and appearance in social interaction. This may have social implications such as 'promiscuous friending' where the network is both a collection of known relationships as well as people with whom users may have never met. Beyond enabling social connections, this could lead to fame seeking or the desire to be 'popular' through the social imaginary of the multimedia environment.

The popularity of such sites may also be explained by the need of some to look into other people's lives or to increase awareness of others within their physical and virtual communities (Straten and Richter 2007: 157). Inherent to such a landscape is the ability to track other members of the community where the 'surveillance' functions allows an individual to track the actions and beliefs of the larger groups to which they belong (Lampe et al. 2006: 167). Lampe et al. (2006) define this as social searching or social browsing where it enables users to investigate specific people with whom they share an offline connection. Lampe et al. (2006: 167) take the relationship between social networking and social browsing further by asserting that 'users largely use social networking to learn more about people they meet offline and are less likely to use the site to initiate new connections.'

Viviane Serfaty (2004) characterises blogs as being, simultaneously, mirrors and veils where we curate ourselves such that our reflections please. There is a duality of revealing and veiling where we may use information selectively to present only certain aspects of ourselves to our audience. The need to constantly curate oneself online has enabled a multitude of behaviours to emerge in terms of notions of vanity, narcissism and self-representation. One study found that millennials spend a great deal of time posting pictures and are quick to remove or untag photographs they find unflattering (Pempek et al. 2009). The sustained effort to present oneself in a positive light has also meant an intense focus on impression management online. With the advent of SNSs with an emphasis on constructing profiles, there has been a proliferation of scholarship on the 'narcissistic turn' online (see Ibrahim 2009; Buffardi and Campbell 2008; Bergman et al. 2011) and equally the digital platform as a space for personal identity construction. Bergman et al. (2011: 706) content that motivations for using SNSs by millennials is often guided by narcissism such as having as many friends on SNSs as possible, wanting their SNS friends to know what they were doing, believing their SNS friends were interested in what they are doing, and having their SNS profiles project a positive image.

SELF-LOVE AND THE GLASS-HOUSE SOCIETY

This being the case, we live in a glass-house society where we can watch others and others can watch us. This glass-house society yields and retains many phenomena through this visibility. Rousseau's village is somewhat transplanted in these sites where people can watch and rate each other. The visibility of our transactions makes it possible to both perform identities and rate others whilst becoming reliant on a peer community and external gaze to validate a sense of self. In reconfiguring the notions of space in the virtual sphere, the internet and the wiring up of the world has led to discussions of the global village. Unlike the absolutist society in seventeenth- and eighteenth-century France, which Rousseau was writing in response to, the internet extends the parameters of gaze, sociability, peer validation and the performance of identity. This expands the magnitude of visibility as well as concepts of sociality, and what is relevant here is the external validation we may seek from social networks where identity may be performed through acts of communication and interaction.

Social scientists have long theorised that identity is constructed through the feedback received from others as one manages impressions during social interactions and reflects upon the appraisals of others (Cooley 1902; Goffman 1959; Mead 1934). During emerging adulthood the most relevant information for the self-presentation of possible selves comes from peers (Grotevant 1987). When emerging adults participate in peer relationships they are presenting themselves to one another, trying out aspects of their identities, confirming or rejecting self-concepts through social feedback, and moving toward identity consolidation in the process (Nurmi 2004).The online platforms are spaces where there is a consciousness we will be consumed and endorsed through a peer economy. SNSs emphasise a profile culture and also the notion of social sharing of private information with peer communities (and beyond). In these sites, peer assessment of us and our self-presentations have vital importance. For self-love here manifests through profile building and equally through our public interactions where these are subject to the external gaze.

The ability to tag photos to profiles and the presence of photo recognition software means that there is a loss of visual anonymity, which can be complemented by new forms of gaze (Monotgomery 2007). As such, publicity (and public labels such as 'friends'), exchange and sharing are integral and definitive parts of the SNS culture where the emphasis is not entirely on the authenticity of the information but the elements of connection and connectivity it can create (Nardi 2005). Technologies allow us to endorse and search for people, while technical features allow us to leave public comments about each other or to 'follow' or 'like' each other. This rating economy is made manifest through verbal and non-verbal features. From searching to tagging to liking and re-posting or re-tweeting we have numerous ways to consume each other and also to endorse or censure each other. The digital sociality of SNSs hinges on peer groups and friends forming a community of connection with one another bound by our banal or eventful life moments. Rousseau's comparative economy is inevitable here but so is the notion of our sense of self emerging and forming through others' valuation of us. As a platform that facilitates UGC, self-representation and the consumption of the self as a commodity by others is a reality in online spaces. Both the peer community and the unknown stranger are one's potential audience. While the notion of narcissism and popularity can go hand in hand, the construction of the virtual self is tied to impression management online (Salimkhan et al. 2010) attributing an intrinsic importance to the concept of self-love in the digital age.

The internet then becomes part of a performance economy where people showcase their intimate lives while projecting material wealth and social status through their lifestyles, consumption patterns and explication of likes and dislikes. This performance culture can project the inequalities in society and between people much more starkly. Performance cultures and the narration of intimate lives online work to highlight both differences and commonalities in peer groups. The emphasis on profile building on SNSs makes people strive to stand out from the rest as an individual.

As Elena Russo (1997: 127) observes, 'the effect of *amour-propre* (or self-love) is thus to create a sort of bondage of the self to the opinion of the public: the self's desire to "make an impression", to appear at its own advantage induces to create an alternative self, more consonant with the expectations of the public'. She argues that this new self is inauthentic because it is imaginary. The discussions of an authentic self take on an added dimension with our transactions in the virtual world particularly with reference to how these converge with our offline selves. While the relationship between morality and authenticity, as opposed to acting to gain peer validation, become composite issues to consider in their own right, it nevertheless stresses the significance of impression management online and the vulnerabilities it produces in the digital economy. Motivations for self-promotion and impression management can induce self-disclosure on SNSs as people seek to impress peers and to relinquish boundaries on what can be disclosed on public platforms (Ibrahim 2008, 2009; Tufekci 2008). As such, amour-propre online can lead to a whole host of behaviours and consequences that can produce foreseen and unforeseen risks for humanity.

We know that SNS communications are different from face-to-face interactions: not only are they disembodied, they are also more public and resonate for longer periods of time (Boyd 2007). Moll et al. (2014) argue that self-disclosure is an important process for building and maintaining ties, especially because it allows for a certain level of trust to be reached, which facilitates the exchange of social capital. While Rousseau was speaking about the risks of vanity and self-love with the emergence of modernity, the online economy capitalises on the politics of self-disclosure through data mining and monetising personal details. Vanity and self-revelation and self-representational models such as interaction through images, text and profiles can be exploited both commercially and through other forms of behaviour, which emerge online. Needless to say this self-disclosure and the need to seek attention and love can be exploited by a wider data economy (Lenhart et al. 2011). Studies have shown that young people divulged private information on personal webpages through their motivations to express themselves and receive self-validation (see Stern 1999, 2004). These data on self-presentation and SNSs coalesce with Buhrmester and Prager's (1995) model for self-disclosure, which posits that adolescents reveal personal information in order to resolve identity issues through peer appraisals. From incursions of privacy to cyber bullying, to the retentive memory of the internet, the vast potential for harm produced by self-revelatory behaviours is still playing out in our contemporary culture. As Bauman (2006) observes, technology engenders a 'moral lag' where we can only comprehend its full implications for humanity retrospectively.

For Rousseau, amour-propre where it is not properly managed can become an obsessive form where self-reflection is stunted and consigned to wanting others to put you above all else. The obsession to have a more superior presence would mean a tendency to court the attention of others and to turn the moral gaze into a space of denigration and humiliation of others. SNSs over the many years since their inception, emergence and domination in our increasingly technologically mediated lives have demonstrated the difficulties presented where peer and friendship groups can quickly disintegrate into denigrative spaces encompassing a range of deviant behaviours including stalking, flaming and cyber bullying. Assessing ourselves through the judgement of our peers then becomes a traumatic phenomenon, which can adversely affect self-worth and self-esteem.

The increasing use of cyberspace as a social networking forum creates a new medium particularly for youth to become victims of peer aggression (Dempsey et al. 2009). Being extremely obsessed with our images and personas online can cause a disconnect between the representations and our real selves. The stress would be on being positively judged by one's peers rather than cultivating and developing virtues in presenting ourselves online and offline. The emphasis on representation can deprive the development of virtues pledging our attention to screen representations divorced from our real selves. The constant need to seek attention from others would create new forms of anxieties in postmodernity where the constant demands of the performative online can erode the therapeutic values of belonging to a community. This can lead to obsessive tendencies, highlighted by Rousseau in his study of modern society, including excessive consumerism and the showcasing of these excesses to online audiences, both friends and strangers. Today our consumerism and fetishes can be instantly profiled to our networked peers making it part of our identity construction.

The gaze of the other here can become a problematic device in such a scenario. Instead of guarding the morality of another, it becomes a means to be cruel and demean others. In such instances, self-love through the evaluation of others becomes a problematic notion in view of the damage such vitriol can cause to one's sense of self. The pledging of self-love to a peer economy presents many issues in our digital culture. Yet it is not possible to live in a vacuum both offline or in a digital environment, and constructive amour-propre would then be dependent on retaining a measure of perspective with regard to peer assessment and evaluations while utilising it productively to check one's moral self.

Screen culture presents many possibilities to represent ourselves and hence self-love online can be performed through a myriad of interactions and we can also assess the attention and validation from our peers through these daily interactions. However, one can't dismiss its damaging and disastrous effects in terms of identity politics where the unforeseen has been evident with deviant behaviours such as cyber bullying and grooming, which have prompted torment, self-harm and suicide.

Self-love can be pledged to a virtuous self and hence self-presentation online can be the basis for the presentation of an authentic self based on these virtues. Beyond performing identities online, one can argue that Rousseau's self-love can yield a more positive society if this self online (or offline) is pegged to a virtuous and moral self. Peers can then accord a form of moral gaze where we can check ourselves through peer evaluations. This peer economy can be part of a wider moral community keeping each other in check whether online or offline particularly when a community or society is faced with trauma or crises that require moral responses to those who are suffering.

Rousseau in highlighting how amour-propre can engender the virtues of pity and empathy with less fortunate human beings also exemplifies how the social self can play an important role as part of a wider community. This is increasingly relevant to the politics of pity online when a society is confronted with a tragedy or crisis. In digital cultures, self-representation online is not unconnected to wider political and social issues including the ability to engage with traumatic issues and to demonstrate pity and solidarity with others (Ibrahim 2010). The visibility of our transactions online requires us to have moral responses to disasters and tragedies. Both self-representation and peer evaluations become part of this public display of pity and communal solidarity. The constant showcasing of communal solidarity and politics of pity is an important renewal of modern and technologically mediated societies, which provides a moral validation of each other as equals and human beings.

In describing Rousseau's concept of natural pity, Dent (1989) observes its relevance in how individuals value each other. For natural man, a similar process of identification occurs as one fully understands the distress that another goes through. The feelings of suffering are very familiar because of similar experiences of being hurt or enduring pain. As a result, this individual is able to recognise and respond better in a spontaneous and compassionate manner to the feelings of others. Natural man empathetically shares the suffering of the individual and attempts to help by alleviating the distress as if the pain was his own (Dent 1989). Today digital cultures offer the possibilities to empathise with suffering and to enact pity or to condemn immoral acts and as such the virtuous self is constantly tested in online spaces. Our ability to show solidarity, grief and memorialise with tragic events is well documented on the internet (see Ibrahim 2015) and as such amour-propre is both intimately implicated in enacting pity for the less fortunate as much as it is about displaying the virtuous self online.

CONCLUSION

The self, through the gaze and validation of others, acquires social capital in online platforms. In tandem, impression management becomes an intrinsic element of digital living, re-asserting the salient concept of self-love and the inherent instabilities it presents. The moral gaze of others can both be a validation and check on the virtuous self. Nevertheless, Rousseau's prophetic caution against self-ruin and social denigration can be further extended to the digital age where an inflamed self-love if unchecked can lead to limitless possibilities for destruction where an obsession with the self and peer validation, and equally a lack of inhibition with what we reveal in curating ourselves can lead to known and unknown risks (Ibrahim 2008). An unchecked amour-propre can not only heighten the inequalities in society but create fragile human relationships where we constantly seek communion with wider communities to validate ourselves and expect them to place us above others. As such it not only raises questions about the authenticity of the self but also the integrity of peer relationships.

The notion of the self on SNSs is both imagined through self-description and crafted through textual and multimedia environments but equally through its articulation and display of contacts and its ability to invite or deny communion with other users. In this sense, the concept of the self is anchored through both individual agency and imagination as well as other users' gaze and consumption of these profiles. This explicit ethos of exposure, display and spectacle define the cultural ethos of SNSs. Self-exposure and narcissism gives a platform for re-definition of offline identities and new sociabilities that can in turn re-configure and re-define the notion of friendship and community in these spaces. SNSs also herald the emergence of complicit risk communities where personal information becomes social capital, which is traded and exchanged and where the concept of public or private can be defined through the nature of users' access, gaze and the transactions and interactions they permit.

The culture of SNSs thrives on the narcissistic and the performative, on one hand, and reciprocity and exchange, on the other. Hence the potential dangers and risks of willingly disclosing and displaying personal details become part of the architecture or code of these sites. The appropriation of new technologies by individuals in order to communicate, to form new communities and to maintain existing relationships signifies new ways in which risk becomes embedded and encoded into our social practices, posing new ethical and legal challenges that inadvertently expand the landscape of risk.

BIBLIOGRAPHY

Aguiar, J.V. (2011). "The Aestheticization of Everyday Life and the De-classicization of Western Working-Classes." *The Sociological Review, 59*(3), 616–632.

Back, M.D., Stopfer, J.M., Vazire, S., Gaddis, S., Schmukle, S.C., Egloff, B., & Gosling, S.D. (2010). "Facebook Profiles Reflect Actual Personality, Not Self-Idealization." *Psychological Science, 21*, 372–374.

Barthes, Roland. 1981. Camera Lucida: Reflections on Photography. Hill and Wang, New York.

Bataille, Georges. ([1949] 1967). *La Part Maudite*. Paris: Editions de Minuit.

Bauman, Z. (2001). *Community*. Cambridge: Polity Press.

Belk, R.W. (2003). "The Fire of Desire: A Multisited Inquiry into Consumer Passion." *Journal of Consumer Research, 30*, 326–351.

Bauman, Z. (2006). *Liquid Fear*. Cambridge: Polity.

Bergman, S.M., Fearrington, M.E., Davenport, S.W., & Bergman, J.Z. (2011). "Millennials, Narcissism, and Social Networking: What Narcissists Do on Social Networking Sites and Why." *Personality and Individual Differences, 50*(5), 706–711.

Bloom, Allan. (1993). "Rousseau and the Romantic Project." In *Love and Friendship*. New York: Simon & Schuster.

Bourdieu, Pierre. 1990. Photography. A Middle-Brow Art. Cambridge: Polity Press.

Boyd, D. (2007). "Social Network Sites: Public, Private, or What?" *Knowledge Tree*, 13. Retrieved March 22, 2010, from http://kt.flexiblelearning.net.au/tkt2007/?page_id=28

Boyd, D., & Heer, J. (2006). "Profiles as Conversation: Networked Identity Performance on Friendster." In *Proceedings of the Hawaii International Conference on System Sciences (HICSS-39)*, Persistent Conversation Track, Kauai, HI: IEEE Computer Society, January 4–7, 2006.

Braidotti, R. (2002). *Metamorphoses: Towards a Materialist Theory of Becoming*. Cambridge: Polity.

Brugger, P. (2002). "Reflective Mirrors: Perspective-Taking in Autoscopic Phenomena." *Cognitive Neuropsychiatry, 7*(3), 179–194.

Buhrmester, D., & Prager, K. (1995). "Patterns and Functions of Self-Disclosure During Childhood and Adolescence." In *Disclosure Processes in Childhood and Adolescence*, edited by K.J. Rotenberg, 10–56. New York: Cambridge University Press.

Buffardi, L.E., & Campbell, W.K. (2008). "Narcissism and Social Networking Websites." *Personality and Social Psychology Bulletin, 34*, 1303–1314.

Chalfen, Richard. 1987. Snapshot Versions of Life. Bowling Green, Ohio: Popular Press.

Cooley, C.H. (1902). *Human Nature and the Social Order*. New York: Charles Scribner's Sons.

Cooper, L.D. (1998). "Rousseau on Self-Love: What We've Learned, What We Might Have Learned." *The Review of Politics, 60*(4), (Autumn, 1998), 661–683.

Cassirer, Ernst. (1951). *The Philosophy of the Enlightenment*. Translated by Fritz C. A. Koel In and James P. Pettegrove. Princeton UP; Boston: Beacon Press, 1955.

Curtin, K. (1996). "Similarities Between Rousseau's Discourse on the Origins of Inequality Among Men and Concepts in Person-Centred Counselling." *The Person-Centred Journal, 3*(1), 15–22.

Davies, Martin L. (1989). "History as Narcissism." *Journal of European Studies, 19*(4), 265–291.

Dempsey, A.G., Sulkowski, M.L., Nichols, R., & Storch, E.A. (2009). "Differences Between Peer Victimization in Cyber and Physical Settings and Associated Psychosocial Adjustment in Early Adolescence." *Psychology in the Schools, 46*(10), 962–972.

Dent, N.J.H., & O'Hagan, T. (1999). "Rousseau on Amour Propre." *Proceedings of the Aristotelian Society*, New Series, *99*(1999), 91–107.

Dent, N.J.H. (1992). *A Rousseau Dictionary*. Oxford, UK: Blackwell Publishers.

Dent, N.J.H. (1989). *Rousseau: An Introduction to His Psychological, Social, and Political Theory*. New York: Basil Blackwell Inc.

Donath, J., & Boyd, D. (2004). "Public Displays of Connection." *BT Technology Journal, 22*(4), 71–81.

Foucault, M. (1986). *The History of Sexuality, Volume Three, The Care of the Self*. Translated by Robert Hurley. New York: Penguin Books. (Trans. of Le Souci de soi. Paris: Editions Gallimard, 1984).

Goffman, E. (1959). *Presentation of Self in Everyday Life*. Garden City, NY: Doubleday Anchor Books.

Grotevant, H.D. (1987). "Toward a Process Model of Identity Formation." *Journal of Adolescent Research, 2*, 203–222.

Harrison, Barbara. 2002. "Everyday photographic practice: People, relationships, networks and "community"." Paper presented at International Visual Sociology Association Conference, Santorini, Greece, July 21–24.

Heeter, C. (1992). "Being There: The Subjective Experience of Presence." *Presence, Teleoperators, and Virtual Environments, 1*, 262–271.

Ibrahim, Y. (2008). "The New Risk Communities: Social Networking Sites and Risk." *International Journal of Media & Cultural Politics, 4*(2), 245–253.

Ibrahim, Yasmin. (2009). "Social Networking Sites (SNS) and the 'Narcissistic Turn'." In *Collaborative Technologies and Applications for Interactive Information Design: Emerging Trends in User Experiences: Emerging Trends in User Experiences*, 82–96.

Ibrahim, Y. (2010). "Distant Suffering and Postmodern Subjectivity: The Communal Politics of Pity." *Nebula, 7*(1–2), 112–135.

Ibrahim, Y. (2015). "Neda, Martyrdom and the Media Event: Death Imagery as an Iconic Memory." *The Poster, 3*(1–2), 31–48.

Jean-Jacques Rousseau. (1964). *The First and Second Discourses.* Edited by Roger D. Masters. Translated by Roger D. Masters & Judith R. Masters. New York: St Martin's Press.

Joinson, A.N. (2008). "Looking at, Looking Up or Keeping Up with People? Motives and Use of Facebook." In *Proceedings of CHI '08*, New York, NY, USA, ACM, pp. 1027–1036.

Kolodny, N. (2010). "The Explanation of Amour Propre." *Philosophical Review, 119*(2), 165–200. http://sophos.berkeley.edu/kolodny/165.pdf

Lampe, C., Ellison, N., & Steinfield, C. (2006). "A Face(book) in the Crowd: Social Searching Vs. Social Browsing." In *CSCW'06*, November 4–8, 2006, Banff, Alberta, Canada.

Lenhart, A, Madden, M., Smith, A., Purcell, K., Zickhur, K., & Raine, L. (2011, November 9). "Teens, Kindness and Cruelty on Social Media." Pew Research Centre. http://www.pewinternet.org/2011/11/09/teens-kindness-and-cruelty-on-social-network-sites/

Madden, M. (2013). "Majority of Online Americans Google Themselves." Pew Research Centre. http://www.pewresearch.org/fact-tank/2013/09/27/majority-of-online-americans-google-themselves/

Martin. (2009). https://ndpr.nd.edu/news/24136-rousseau-s-theodicy-of-self-love-evil-rationality-and-the-drive-for-recognition/

Manago, A., Graham, M., Greenfield, P., & Salimkhan, G. (2008). "Self-Presentation and Gender on MySpace." *Journal of Applied Developmental Psychology, 29*, 446–458.

Mead, G.H. (1934). *Mind, Self, and Society.* Chicago: University of Chicago Press.

Michel de Montatgne. (1948). "On Vanity." In *The Complete Essays of Montaigne.* Translated by Donald Frame, 729. Stanford: Stanford University Press.

McLendon, M.L. (2003). "The Overvaluation of Talent: An Interpretation and Evaluation of Amour Propre." *Polity, 36*(1), 115–138.

McNichol, T. (2009, April 25). "Why Google Wants You to Google Yourself." Time.com. http://content.time.com/time/business/article/0,8599,1893965,00.html

Moll, R. Pieschl, S., & Bromme, R. (2014). "Trust into Collective Privacy? The Role of Subjective Theories for Self-Disclosure in Online Communication." *Societies, 4,* 770–784.

Monotgomery, E. (2007). "Facebook: Fraudsters Paradise?" Money.UK.MSN. Com. 20 Nov 2007. Retrieved December 4 2007, from http://money.uk.msn. com/banking/id-fraud/article.aspx?cp-documentid=5481130

Nardi, B. A. (2005). Beyond bandwidth: Dimensions of connection in interpersonal communication. Computer Supported Cooperative Work (CSCW), 14(2), 91–130.

Nurmi, J. (2004). "Socialization and Self-Development. Channeling, Selection, Adjustment, and Reflection." In *Handbook of Adolescent Psychology*, edited by R. Lerner & L. Steinberg, 85–124, 2nd ed. Hoboken, NJ: John Wiley & Sons.

O'Shea, Anthony. (2002), "Desiring Desire: How Desire Makes Us Human, All Too Human." *Sociology, 26*(November), 925–940.

Pempek, T.A., Yermolayeva, Y.A., & Calvert, S.L. (2009). "College Students' Social Networking Experiences on Facebook." *Journal of Applied Developmental Psychology, 30*(3), 227–238.

Rose, Gillian. 2003. "Family Photography and Domestic Spacings: A Case Study." Transactions of the Institute of British Geographers, 28(1): 5–18.

Rosen, C. (2007). "Virtual Friendship and the New Narcissism." *The New Atlantis, 17,* 15–31.

Russo, E. (1997). *The Self, Real and Imaginary: Social Sentiment in Marivaux and Hume.* Edited by Elena Russo, Yale French Studies, 92, Exploring the Conversible World: Text and Sociability from the Classical Age to the Enlightenment, 126–148.

Rousseau, J.J. (1984). *A Discourse on Inequality.* Translated by M. Cranston. London: Penguin Books. (Original work published 1755).

Salimkhan, G., Manago, A., & Greenfield, P. (2010). "The Construction of the Virtual Self on MySpace." *Cyberpsychology: Journal of Psychosocial Research on Cyberspace, 4*(1), article 1. http://cyberpsychology.eu/view.php?cisloclanku=2 010050203&article=1

Second Discourse, in First and Second Discourses. Translated by Roger D. Masters & Judith R. Masters (New York: St. Martin's Press, 1964), 221–222.

Starobinski, J. (1988). *Jean-Jacques Rousseau, Transparency and Obstruction.* Chicago: University of Chicago.

Serfaty, V. (2004). *The Mirror and the Veil: An Overview of American Online Diaries and Blogs.* Amsterdam Monographs in American Studies, Amsterdam.

Strater, K., & Richter, H. (2007). "Examining Privacy and Disclosure in a Social Networking Community." In *Symposium on Usable Privacy and Security (SOUPS) 2007*, July 18–20, 2007, Pittsburgh, PA, USA.

Sreenivasan, S. (2013, October 15). "How Googling Others Affects Voting, Hiring and Dating." CNet.com. http://www.cnet.com/uk/news/how-googling-others-affects-voting-hiring-and-dating/

Stefanone, M., Lackoff, D., & Rosen, D. (2008). "We're All Stars Now: Reality Television, Web 2.0, and Mediated Identities." In *HT'08*, June 19–21, Pittsburgh, Pennsylvania, USA.

Stern, S.R. (1999). "Adolescent Girls' Expression on Web Home Pages: Spirited, Somber and Self- Conscious Sites." *Convergence: The Journal of Research into New Media Technologies, 5*, 22–41.

Stern, S.R. (2004). "Expressions of Identity Online: Prominent Features and Gender Differences in Adolescents' World Wide Web Home Pages." *Journal of Broadcasting & Electronic Media, 48*, 218–243.

Siibak, A. (2009). "Constructing the Self Through the Photo Selection – Visual Impression Management on Social Networking Websites." *Cyberpsychology: Journal of Psychosocial Research on Cyberspace, 3*, article 1.

Tufekci, Z. (2008). "Can You See Me Now? Audience and Disclosure Regulation in Online Social Network Sites." *Bulletin of Science, Technology & Society, 28*, 20–36.

Valkenburg, P.M., Jochen, P., & Schouten, A.P. (2006). "Friend Networking Sites and Their Relationship to Adolescents' Well-Being and Self-Esteem." *Cyberpsychology & Behavior, 9*, 584–590.

Zhao, S., Grasmack, S., & Martin, J. (2008). "Identity Construction on Facebook: Digital Empowerment in Anchored Relationships." *Computers in Human Behavior, 24*, 1816–1836.

Self-Commodification and Value

Abstract The self confronts capital directly in the online environment. While the self is a constant source of data, revenue and content for capital, it would be too limiting to imagine the self solely as an entity to create value online. This chapter examines the relationship between self and capital and how the politics of self-production feeds numerous strands of e-commerce online while enabling therapeutic and empowering elements for the self. The relationship between the self and capital enters a complicit arrangement where the insatiable appetite for non-events and non-news drives an economy of attention seeking and deriving pleasure from the banal.

Keywords Capital • Social capital • Value • Co-Creation • Self-Commodification

Introduction

According to Mead (1934: 138), 'the essential problem of self-hood or of self-consciousness' is for the individual to 'get outside himself (experientially) in such a way as to become an object to himself'. In the multitude of representational modes that online platforms present, the self as an entity becomes commodified and enters into a complex relationship with capital and forms of gaze. The advent of vlogs and the proliferation of interactive and spectacular platforms showcase people's everyday lives and

© The Author(s) 2018
Y. Ibrahim, *Production of the 'Self' in the Digital Age*,
https://doi.org/10.1007/978-3-319-74436-0_4

allow for consumption to be enacted publicly. This has meant the self is intimately implicated as a commercial entity in platforms that can enable advertising aimed at niche audiences. The self enters into realms of publicness where it is constituted through its consumption by others, through both their gaze and engagements. In terms of popular imagination, this offers the potential for ordinary people to become a 'celebrity', to have a fan base and to be commented on and subscribed to while casting the self into new modes of engagement and entanglements through acts of watching. The self as a co-creator with a multitude of agents and an internet architecture is seen not as neutral but extracted to produce value and to be relentlessly converted into data.

This insertion of a self into a generative economy that is hungry for content, data assemblages and a virality designed to cater to an attention economy casts the self into a composite array of phenomena. The insertion of self onto the screen and its spectacular economy has been a source of critical academic debates. Marxist critiques of the internet speak of the ways in which digital platforms extract immaterial labour and surplus value from the self such that it is a vulnerable entity performing to the lure of capital. The juxtaposition of the self with capital casts it through a long trajectory of labour struggles with capital where the self is seen through surplus labour and a false economy of empowerment. But through its long history of entanglement with capital's extraction of value from labour, the architecture of the internet induces new forms of vulnerabilities and risk. This commodification of the self can be understood through its movements as data, whether big data or personalised and customised data. The self can be converted and enmeshed with algorithms and popular consumption practices that can re-craft it as a commodity that can yield value while being amenable to the accumulation of social capital in its own right. The entrapment of the self within the critical Marxist paradigms of exploitation of labour on the one hand, and the self as vulnerable to the architecture of data extraction and virality on the other, position value as externalised. Value is produced and given to others and I'd like to explore self-commodification through its transformations through the screen and through the Derridean idea of constituting the self through others by drawing on Levinas.

The automatic mining of personal and behavioural data is arguably a platform owner's most important driver for promoting online traffic; at the same time, standardising data input guarantees better results. If users' input is channelled through formatted interfaces, it enhances a

site's connective potential. The 'connective turn' in social media came with a noticeable shift in the organisation of platforms from database structures into narrative structures. José van Dijck (2013: 203) drawing on Lev Manovich (2001) points out that the Web 2.0 in its early years, can be understood as databases or 'organised collections of textual, audio-visual and numerical data supported by a database management system. Unlike previous media-interactive platforms that forced users to present information in a non-linear, non-narrative fashion, databases do not tell stories with a beginning or end'. Without a system to organise these elements into a sequence the user interface of digital media becomes highly dependent on search systems to retrieve data (Manovich 2001: 322–3).

The commodification of the self should not be collapsed into a duality of exploitation or empowerment such that the self is imprisoned through pervasive exploitation and risk landscapes flattening the textured terrain of experiences that unfold through the screen. It is worth considering that the enmeshing of the performative, spectacular, and celebrification and the experiencing of the self through a plethora of activities from activism to the emergence of new visual cultures produces new conventions of communicating and experiencing the self and its relationship with a wider community of consumers and in tandem consumption economies. Thus the phenomenon of self-commodification can showcase the relationships that currently exist between the dominant mode of production and its modes of subjection (Read 2003) but equally the emergence of popular practices and conventions of experience constitute and enact the self. This prosumer capitalism is perceived as a shift away from manual labour to creative labour (Ritzer 2015) and folding these modes of engagement into labour practices or in terms of surplus value delimit the scope and dimensions that compose the self as commodity and value online.

The Self as a Commodity of Exchange and Value

John Locke (cf. Mitchell 1986) envisaged the self as a form of property subject to market exchange. With the collapsing of boundaries between the consumer and producer, the users become re-birthed as 'prosumers', which invites a proliferation of discourses about agency and empowerment of audiences in the digital age. The transition from the static World Wide

Web to Web 2.0 with multimedia forms meant that the self could be re-presented and visualised through these new digital platforms through technological convergence. This brought the corporeal body into constant interplay with the new media technologies facilitating endless possibilities to re-brand the self as a commodity, to co-create desire and to be consumed by others. The self as an entity produced through multimedia platforms that were being inserted into new forms of labour economies to release value brought renewed critical discourses highlighting the exploitation of immaterial labour. As such, the concept of virtuosity in Marxist critiques becomes a core component of immaterial labour under post-Fordism (see Lazzarato 1996).

The architecture of the World Wide Web is such that it atomises data trails from the disembodied transactions of the self. The self goes through a re-calibration of its existence where something called data is extracted relentlessly. This means the self as an entity is prone to visible and invisible process of exploitation through its movements online, igniting various phenomena within the architecture of the Word Wide Web—whether this be data trails or images that are pulled into a virality of circulation where they can exist stripped from context. This commodification of the self is multifaceted. One the one hand, it enters into new kinds of transaction with capital where its performance and production capacities can reach a new market and be amenable to new audiences. It can be inserted into niche attention economies online but it can equally be extracted and sold as data to third parties with or without consent. This constant entanglement with the commercialised World Wide Web, which is reliant on user engagement, user feedback and user-generated content makes the production of self a phenomenon that performs various tasks and functions online.

There is a proliferation of literature that has sought to view the co-optation of the self into modes of cultural production and labour through an array of terms that reveal an entanglement of the self with capital. Prahalad and Ramaswamy (2000) spoke of the 'productive customers' involved in the process of 'co-creation' where consumers co-operate with firms in the creation of value. This process of co-operation has also been viewed as a 'service-dominant logic' of economic exchange (Vargo and Lusch 2004) to underscore the consumer as a 'co-producer' in the value and service chain. The concept of 'working consumer' (Cova and Dalli 2009) was deployed to analyse consumers who participate in the value-creation process through immaterial labour.

Alison Hearn (2008) defines self-branding as involving the self-conscious construction of the self through the use of cultural meanings and images drawn from the narrative and visual codes of the mainstream culture industries (2008: 198). Hearn (2008: 198), drawing on Giddens, argues that the project of the self in modernity is a distinct form of labour. As such the production of self must always involve some form of labour in order to create a public persona that might be of practical or relational use (2008: 214). As such the self is a site for the extraction of value. Hearn (2008: 203), in drawing on David Harvey (1990) and Luc Boltanski and Eve Chiapello (2002), discusses self-branding through the shifts in capital accumulation in response to the economic crises of the 1970s. There is now is less reliance on concrete material production and more on the production and consumption of knowledge and symbolic products emphasising packaging, image, design and marketing. This flexible accumulation of capital as such premises on strategies of permanent innovation, mobility and change where sub-contracting and spontaneous collaborations become part of this enterprise. The centring of creativity as such is seen as a means to counter earlier criticisms about capital's alienation and disenfranchisement of labour.

Tiziana Terranova (2000) contends that the internet does not automatically turn every user into an active producer and every worker into a creative subject. The process whereby production and consumption are re-configured within the category of free labour signals the unfolding of a different (rather than completely new) logic of value, whose operations need careful analysis (Terranova 2000: 36). This process is thus socially shaped not a deterministic model of people working because capital wants them, and there is a need to recognise their desire for affective and cultural production as real. These configurations posit the digital economy as a space of intense experimentation that is not only concerned to forms of production but also the emergence of new forms of activities that we may not categorise outright as labour. These modes of cultural production and labour have not developed in direct response to the economic needs of capital. Instead, Terranova (2000: 36) attributes it to the expansion of the cultural industries and as part of a process of economic experimentation with the creation of monetary value out of knowledge/culture/affect. In these processes, there is a channelling of collective labour into the monetary flows within capitalist business practices.

ENACTING 'VALUE' THROUGH THE SPECTACULAR AND THE PERFORMATIVE

The notion of value within the Marxist critique of 'prosumerism' and 'co-creation' produces a rhetoric in which the self is exploited, vulnerable and enmeshed through a false economy of empowerment. This flattens both the landscape of the internet and the forms of activities that occur on it. Without doubt, over the years, the internet has become increasingly commercialised with increased data analysis of people's movement and with the overarching economy of search engines that order information and knowledge. Nevertheless, the self enacted through a multitude of activities and compositions including gaming sites and second screens where it views itself through avatars, requires a textured approach to the production of self. Sociologists point out that the self has become a major source of investment and labour in modernity. There is some intense and sustained labour necessary in crafting the self, making it a 'reflexive project' in modernity (Giddens 1991). For Giddens (1991) the constitution of the self entails a dynamic interplay between agency and structure under the conditions of high modernity such that it acquires the role of a project to be continuously worked entailing both abstract systems and concrete structures. The rise of individualisation and expansion of the digital economy are seen as part of the characteristics of late modernity (Giddens 1991). The rise of new media technologies such as search engines and networking sites are also seen as undermining social relations and the self (Bauman 2003). These discourses draw on Heidegger's notion that technology and society are the conditions of possibility for each other (1977).

Beck (2001) for his part, depicts a social landscape in which, following the decline of tradition and the social welfare state, the individual has been isolated as the main bearer of responsibility for his or her own fate such that the ethics of individual self-fulfilment and achievement becomes an important strand in modern society. According to Beck (2001: 22), the 'human being who aspires to be the author of his or own life, the creator of individual identity, is the central character of our time'. Beck (2001: 26) contends that the typical modern mass media with its centralised and paternalistic organisation fails to equip properly the pursuits of the reflexive self that require 'processing of contradictory information, dialogue, negotiation, compromise'. The conditions of modernity and the resources that surround humans including the symbolic then become materials for self-construction and representation. For Thompson (1995) the process of self-formation throughout modernity has been increasingly enhanced through mediated symbolic materials, greatly expanding the range of options available to individuals.

Technology is one of the many things through which identity is constructed. The modern approach to identity arose due to a 'wide range of practices – religious, political, economic, familial, intellectual, artistic – converged and reinforced each other to produce it' (Taylor 1989: 206). The emergence of identities online did not necessarily mean that this identity stood apart from offline identities. How these identities enmeshed became strands of renewed academic enquiry but nevertheless the digital self emerged as part of identity construction particularly with a recognition that we possess multiple identities rather than a unitary self. The increased commercialisation of the internet and the intense consumerism, along with the conversion of human enterprise and sociality online into data designed to market goods and services, highlights the ways in which the self is given to the designs of capital. But to read the self predominantly through this paradigm collapses the reading into one of exploitation alone. I want to explore other concepts such as performativity, agency and social capital that layer the construction of the self online despite the dominance of the commercial agenda.

Postmodernism characterises the self as an ephemeral, liquid image, tossed, turned and decentred by rampant consumerism and disembodied electronic media (Gubrium and Holstein 1995: 555). The self, in constituting itself through digital platforms, lends itself to new formats both discursive and visual, including the symbolic. The screen as a conveyor of intense desire, spectacle, forms of mobility and voyeurism forges an intimate relationship with the corporeal body through wearable technologies and equally through its presence in our domestic settings. The screen in enabling presence without embodiment means that the self as an entity is again reconfigured through pixels, data, bitmaps and algorithms online. The production of the self online means that it is converted into new formats in different online spaces. It is difficult to conceive the self as unitary as it is projected onto many platforms through its engagement online. Everything from information seeking, knowledge creation, consumerism and activism happens on the internet. The self can be converted into semantic words, images, emoticons and so forth. In fact, the self is not a unitary entity online. In moving from the online to offline, a technical transformation happens to the self where there is a conversion of what is believed to be an 'inner essence' into technical formats. The self pulled away from the body and inserted into the virtual goes through a transformative process as it gets entangled in a public gaze and confronts the hand of capital. The virality of the medium and its circulation modes mean that the self becomes transformed in terms of its having a 'technical' presence as opposed to just being an inner essence. More importantly, the projection of the self through the screen making it consumable by the embodied self offline is unsettling. This splitting of the self through modes of self-expression online means that the data or digital self is uncoupled in manifest ways from its embodied self. This screen (that doubles the self and splits it into a digital self) unlike that of television or cinema, forges a new relationship with the self. It affords new ways of thinking and rumination about what could constitute consciousness including the idea of humans becoming 'post-human', where we can transcend time and space, to be crafted without meat or flesh and to be implicated in futuristic ways to live through the immateriality of cyberspace. The possibilities to imagine the human as post-human or to be a part of networks means the self and its corporeal emphasis shifts to other formats such as the dataset giving rise to new forms of control and appropriation to be culled, extrapolated and appropriated as big data where we swim with different patterns of sense and meaning making. Digital tools help shape how we imagine ourselves in our daily lives from webcamming to geolocative tracking. By performing through these diverse range of sites and platforms people are able to visualise themselves in new forms of reality and hypervisibility.

Since the 1990s post-structuralist and feminist theory have conceived subjectivity as fluid and contingent enacted through historical and cultural frameworks marking a shift from Enlightenment perspectives of viewing identity as a core inner essence that manifests through behaviour and discourse. The insertion and re-configuration of the self through technology and the screen means the self is crafted through digital architecture and its interface situating the self as decentred from the corporeal and that which can be enacted through the screen to produce affective and haptic experiences. In contrast with the Enlightenment paradigm of a unitary entity, the self becomes decentred and atomised through these 'technologies of self' (Foucault). To consign the self through the concept of value delimits it as labour and commodity for capital, casting it as vulnerable and in linear deterministic modes to be ultimately exploited. It equally counters the postmodern notion of identities as fluid by consigning every enterprise online as forms of 'labour'. This polysemic and floating character of the 'postmodern media self' implicates it through its local interpretive practices, in which individuals actively represent and manage their identities (Featherstone 1988: 206). It is problematic to render this activity completely to the workings of capital alone.

Much of postmodern scholarship assumes a radical anti-essentialism that rejects, on philosophical grounds, the very concept of self (Callero 2003: 116). The fluid self of postmodernity appropriates resources of its everyday experiences to produce identity and as such its performativity is about both agency and its constraints, and equally the potential to create social capital. While Enlightenment discourses constructed the romantic self as being an essence, unified and autonomous, feminist philosophy and politics, on the other hand, advocate the self as gendered. The binding of the self with one identity or reading as a completed ontological entity has been resisted over time. Edward Said (1994) objects to the construction of the single identity asserting that a person does not remain a particular kind of self forever, ontologically and epistemologically. With notions of identity not as singular but plural and defined not by sameness but difference, psychology has turned its attention to multiple identities (Rosenberg 1986). The contemporary self is depicted as fragmented (Jameson 1985), essentially fluid and many-sided. Stephen Greenblatt (2, 257) in his theory of self-fashioning describes 'an increased self-consciousness about the fashioning of human identity as a manipulable, artful process'. The readings of self as an exploited entity alone again reduce the possibilities in which there is agency and constraints in the construction of the self.

For Foucault, the self is the direct consequence of power traced and apprehended through historically specific systems of discourse. These regimes of power bring the self into existence by imposing disciplinary practices on the body. Through the technologies of surveillance, measurement, assessment and classification of the body, the subject comes into existence through systems of discourse. The subject as a product of networks of power and discourse is not analysed as the source and foundation of knowledge. Foucault (1980) in 'The Eye of Power' locates the gaze within an apparatus of power relations. Power functions optimally when those who are imprisoned come to guard their own actions, to embrace the logic of surveillance in which they are caught and by which they are defined. The gaze then functions to 'self-regulate'. Foucault in *Discipline and Punish*, discusses the growth of productive technologies of power where these were focused on the body as an object and target of power through institutionalised gaze where the art of the human body was revived as a whole anatomo-politics (Rayner 2001: 148).

Within the settings of the internet, its role for surveillance and monitoring as part of a wider data economy is a well-established trope. It not possible to conceive the internet as a space without a surveillance mechanism and hence despite earlier discourses of freedom, information and emancipation of the internet as a space where communication flows may circumnavigate the traditional models of dissemination, there is cognisance that the architecture of the World Wide Web and its control and regulation can coalesce with the exiting modes of power. As such the early discourses of freedom and liberation gave way to a more cautious self that had to craft itself through a sustained process of negotiations with the architecture of the internet, regulations, states and authorities. The self could be mined not just for commercial operations but by states and governments as part of an increased agenda of securitisation.

Foucault (1988: 18) defines technologies of the self as a suite of technologies that permit individuals to affect by their own means, or with the help of others, a certain number of operations on their own bodies and souls, thoughts, conduct and way of being, so as to transform themselves in order to attain a certain state of happiness, purity, wisdom, perfection or immortality. Technologies of the self should not be conceptualised in isolation, as these are constituted through a larger family of technologies including technologies of production, technologies of sign systems and technologies of power. These types of technologies, Foucault (1988: 18) maintains, 'hardly ever function separately, but each plays a key part in the constitution of human beings and requires the individual's specific modification through training and the acquisition of specific skills and attitudes'. Foucault's notion of technologies of self has stressed the issues of domination and power but nevertheless there is acknowledgement about the interaction between oneself and others. Despite the emphasis on the strong relation with domination, there is some recognition of the active engagement on the part of the subject and their agency (Sawicki 1996: 174–177). Another distinct aspect of the technologies of the self is the possibility of interaction of some sort between the self and the public.

The implication of the construction of the self evident in Foucault's technologies of the self is also an important dimension in the theories of symbolic interactionism where there is a perennial flow of meaningful symbols between 'I' and others as the main driver of the emergence of 'me' or the socialised self (Mead 1934). The sociality of the internet means the self is consciously performed by individuals where the 'I' is entangled with its consumption by others. Hence the dramaturgical model of the presentation of the self (Goffman 1959) is inscribed through the screen and the possibilities for multimedia formats for self-representation. This presentational self online encompasses a wider array of phenomena including power relations, social historicity of technology and the material instrumentality of platforms. These processes can impose different forms of subjectivity on the self. The notion of technology of the self thus has to integrate various phenomena along with the performative dimensions of the self in everyday settings.

In drawing on Judith Butler's notion of performativity to social networking sites (SNSs), Rob Cover (2012) highlights identity as behaviour, communication, articulation and activity that can be understood as constituting rather than merely representing identity and selfhood. Cover in acknowledging Butler's contribution as complex and wide, explores how the self can be re-constituted or re-configured differently in the encounter with new and imaginative discursive arrangements (Butler 1991: 18). By employing Butler's theories of performative identity, Cover argues that the uses of SNSs are performative acts in and of themselves and bases it on the idea that identity and subjectivity are ongoing processes of becoming, rather than an ontological state of being (Butler 1990). The process of subject formation is driven by a desire for self-identity.

Butler's theory of performativity seeks to explain how the subversion of power emerges within a dialectical relation between constraint and agency. Butler's description of the contradictory process of social structuration provides an insight into the links between personal and social identity. Performativity than alludes to the culturally crafted aspect of identity generated through repeated conventions that enact power arrangements in society and equally through their transgressions. Subjectification is then not something permanent or stable but contested through inscription of power and resistance against it. Butler's view of self concerns the performative in storytelling and, relatedly, the narrator's reflexivity with the meanings they employ to convey their story. For Judith Butler 'if I question the regime of truth, I question too, the regime through which being, and my own ontological status, is allocated' (2005: 23).

Long before the emergence of online communication, Erving Goffman (1959) theorised self-presentation as a performance; the need for a multiple, composite self has only increased since public communication moved to an online space. Goffman's dramaturgical approach as a metaphorical technique sought to explain how individuals present an 'idealised' as opposed to an authentic version of the self. 'Life becomes a stage for performances where these activities occurs during a period marked by his continuous presence before a particular set of observers and which has some influence on the observers' (1959: 22). The staging of life enables participants to tweak their behaviour and to be engaged in 'impression management'.

The symbolic interactionist school and Irving Goffman view performativity as a form of impression management and structured improvisation through which human beings articulate their purposes, situations and relationships in everyday social life (Schieffelin 1998: 195). For Goffman (1959), human intentionality, culture and social reality are fundamentally articulated through the world through performativity. Goffman's performativity thesis remains vitally important in the digital age as the self is performed through the screen. Goffman also locates self-construction as a matter of everyday work. Csikszentmihalyi and Rochberg-Halton (1981) view household objects, for instance, as actual sources of self-construction. The screen is then part of the domestication of technologies and constitutes everyday living, and the agency of the self can be located through the ordinary flows of life. These ordinary features of everyday life provide the substance of meaning from which individual selves are constructed (Gubrium and Holstein 1995: 555).

The self in contemporary life is constructed in practice akin to Claude Levi-Strauss' process of 'bricolage', in which agency is produced from what is enduringly available. The ordinary mundane elements and circumstances of the everyday are cast as a site for selfconstruction. In the course of everyday life, individuals adroitly construct selves using locally available and meaningful materials shaped on the specifications and demands of the interpretive task at hand. For symbolic interactionists, the self is first and foremost a reflexive process of social interaction. The reflexive process refers to the uniquely human capacity to become an object to one's self, to be both subject and object. Reflexivity is not a biological given but rather emerges from the social experience. It has become common in reviews of the sociological self to argue that the formation of the self is both a social product and a social force (Rosenberg 1986).

The self-concept defined as the totality of the individual's thoughts and feelings with reference to the self as an object (Rosenberg 1986), is a product of various self-objectification processes. Self-objectification is not an innate property of the human organism and emerges through the processes of social interaction with the environment encompassing animate and inanimate entities. The self develops over time through the course of social experience and as such different aspects of the self come to be objectified through the phases of its development. According to the geneticist Theodosius Dobzhansky (1964), the human self-concept is 'man's chief evolutionary novelty'. For Mead, self-objectification was one of the human being's most distinctive qualities and possessed evolutionary significance. Mead (1934: 136) contents that 'Man's behaviour is such in his social group that he is able to become an object to himself, a fact which constitutes him a more advanced product of evolutionary development than are the lower animals. Fundamentally it is this social fact ... that differentiates him from them.'

Van Dijck (2013: 200) in exploring the struggles between users and platforms to control online identities, argues that these struggles are played out at the level of the interface. He points out that after 2008, most 'corporate site owners shifted their focus from running community-oriented platforms to monetising connectivity by maximising lucrative data traffic between people, things and ideas. Along with this shift came a change in platforms' architectures; rather than being databases of personal information they became tools for (personal) storytelling and narrative self-presentation' (Van Dijck 2013: 200). Bruner (1997: 148), in pursuing the wider question of why 'we are compelled to create autobiographic self-narratives observes that self-narratives function to sustain a sense of predictable understanding in the world. When disruption is perceived explained narratives provide a framework for meaning making. Everyone wants to write because everyone has a need to be meaningful to signify what they experience. Otherwise it all slips away'.

Goffman's notion of multiple levels of identity is displayed through the negotiation with this interface with technology. This technological interface can promote both conscious and unconscious modes of self-representation. Goffman's conscious and unconscious levels of self-performance become relevant with this discussion of the interface. While data profiles can be constructed through the architecture of the World Wide Web, users can consciously create their profiles. The exhibition of the self becomes a means to produce social capital. The personal and behavioural data equally provides advertisers with valuable resources to exploit for their own ends. The more connections users make to both human and nonhuman entities, the more social capital they accumulate and the more social capital people assign to things and ideas, the more economic capital can be gained from connectivity (Van Dijck 2013: 202, See also Ellison et al. 2007).

The internet as a digital platform for interactive, multimedia content that works to the processes of convergence and as resources for self-construction are conceptually diverse and include facilities for storytelling, cultural narratives, visual repositories and audience feedback. The digital platforms as such provide a range of cultural tools to develop and maintain various cultural spheres of meaning. Charles Cooley's (1902) notion of the 'looking-glass self' highlights the way the self develops in relation to how we imagine our appearance in the eyes of others. Others are seen as 'mirrors' that reflect the images of the self. Our self-evaluations are affected by the evaluations of others and how we perceive those evaluations. New communication technologies have expanded access to a wide range of generalized others, thus altering 'the backdrop against which identity is constructed' (Cerulo 1997: 397). The influence of technological apparatuses can be seen in the establishment of 'media communities' that add a new dimension to the physical and symbolic environment of our everyday lives (Altheide 2000). Mead (1934) contends that in the process of interacting with different people you encounter a variety of perspectives, interests, attitudes and objectives that may not always be convergent with yours. This realisation that you are both similar to and at the same time different from others serves to define and refine the major aspects of your sense of identity.

Knorr Cetina (2001: 525) in examining the sociological implications of a post-social environment, argues that the individualisation process of modernity empties out traditional forms of sociality by creating space for non-human social resources. She contends that 'the modern untying of identities has been accompanied by an expansion of object-centred environments which situate and stabilise selves, defining individual identity just as much as communities and families used to do'. As such objects come to serve as a resource for identity creation and new communication technologies along with their immateriality as well as virtuality are increasingly implicated in the formation of self.

Beyond agency, the internet also functions as a space for manifest and symbolic forms of self-expression to become a space for witnessing the self. Sartre in his analysis of writing speaks about writing primarily as an existential and private urge for self-proof, a written signification of who or what one believes one is. In calling attention to the meaningfulness of the writing in evidencing the self, Sartre situates writing as an act of bearing witness to oneself. Sartre provokes the notion of self as a dialectic site within which personal production of meanings is discoverable, and writing becomes a witness to one's 'me'. Similarly, for Bakhtin, as one cannot even really see one's own exterior and comprehend it as a whole, and no mirrors

or photographs can help, our real exterior can be seen and understood only by other people, because they are located outside us in space and because they are others (cf. Todorov 1984: 6–7). For Sartre every single person feels, perhaps only unconsciously, the need to be a witness of his time, of his life before the eyes of all, to be a witness to himself (Sartre 1974: 30–32). In a prosumer platform, such as the internet, with its facilities for interactivity, audience and community creation and in interceding through visual, symbolic and creative formats online assists in the construction of a self that is less bound by place (Meyrowitz 1997). As a disembodied presence online, the offline self can watch the self online. In some instances this takes the form of a 'parallel life' as in the case of internet users who engage in extensive, online role-playing games (Turkle 1995) where actors feel liberated in their opportunity to express different 'aspects of the self'.

As the possibilities for self-expression and self-representation expand with new media technologies, the modes for controlling and dominating it also unfold in tandem whether in the guise of cookies, algorithms or moderators. The self then becomes complicit in signing user agreements where it is sold as data to third parties or becomes commodified for advertisers. As such the self labours for itself to create social capital but it is equally being extrapolated into a commercial economy where it creates and commodifies identity images that benefit a consumer economy. The self as complicit, cognitive and resistant of the dialectical aspects of the internet is seen through self-regulation but also in exploiting the platform for self-branding and image management. The role of non-human resources and electronic technologies in constructing the self as a prominent feature of postmodernity is evident here. It resonates with Baudrillard's (1983) argument about societies placing increasing attention on onscreen images.

Beyond narrating the self through economic value, the self has been increasingly understood through the creation of social capital. Bourdieu and Wacquant (1992: 14) define social capital as 'the sum of the resources, actual or virtual, that accrue to an individual or a group by virtue of possessing a durable network of more or less institutionalized relationships of mutual acquaintance and recognition'. Similarly, Coleman (1988) describes social capital as resources accumulated through the relationships between people. The social network as yielding social capital arising from investments in social relations with expected returns (Lin 1999: 30) has been explored in the context of the internet with Castells' notion of the 'network society'. In a network society benefits accrue from the increased access to use of resources embedded in these networks.

Bourdieu and Coleman emphasise the intangible nature of social capital relative to other forms. While economic capital may be about assets such as people's bank accounts and human capital is inside people's heads, social capital relates to others and it is those others, not himself or herself, who are the actual source of his or her advantages (Portes 1998). Portes points out that the classical roots of social capital can be traced to Durkheim's (1893) theory of social integration and the sanctioning capacity of group rituals. Here reciprocity of exchanges, the motivation of donors of socially mediated gifts becomes instrumental. But the expectation of repayment is not based on knowledge of the recipient, but on the insertion of both actors in a common social structure.

At the individual level, social capital allows individuals to capitalise on their connections with others, accruing benefits such as information or support. Putnam (2000) has distinguished between bonding and bridging social capital. Bonding social capital is found between individuals in tightly knit, emotionally close relationships, such as family and close friends. Bridging social capital, on the other hand, emerges from 'weak ties', which are loose connections between individuals who may provide useful information or new perspectives for one another but typically not emotional support (Granovetter 1983). Bridging social capital might be augmented by SNSs as they enable users to create and maintain larger, diffuse networks of relationships from which they could potentially draw resources (Steinfield et al. 2008). Although bridging social capital is viewed as an individual-level construct, prior research has conceptualised it in a community context (Putnam 2000; Williams 2006). These intangible and communal aspects of social capital mean that people view themselves as part of a broader group and exhibit norms of giving within a wider community in the construct. Interactive technologies that facilitate group participation through features such as distribution lists, photo directories, and search capabilities enable the formation of new forms of social capital and the sustenance of relationship building over time more easily and cheaply (Resnick 2001; Donath and Boyd 2004).

The Digital Self

Our selves online as part of our multiple identities bring renewed attention to the issue of labour, aesthetics and therapeutic benefits including the exercise of agency and experiences of communality and publicness that the digital environment affords and facilitates. As Haraway (1991) points out, it is not about finding or re-asserting the boundaries of human/ machine or other so-called oppositions, such as material/imagined, mind/ body. The ontology of the human–technology relation produces a 'world picture' (Heidegger 1977). As posited by Heidegger, the technology of the modern age is deeply implicated in a historically contingent under-standing of world 'beingness' and the human subject.

We are complicit with capital yet not completely unaware of how we can be relentlessly pulled and crafted through a digital economy, hungry for content creation and in distributing the human self through its varied permutations online. Building public profiles and being constantly engaged in the creation of the online selves implicates the everyday and our immediate environment. From a social interactionism perspective we employ the resources from our immediate environments to construct our selves and as such the appropriation of technologies into our everyday lives and domestic environment as well as our corporeal body syncs technolo-gies with the biorhythms of the body and the everyday, where time and space can be re-configured and manipulated. It lends to narratives of human agency and creativity. The doubling of the self in viewing it through online and offline modes creates debates about our congruence with our online selves and about issues of authenticity and its public display. Here its configuration into capital modes of production or the commodification and consumerism become aspects of self-construction, along with human endeavour to perform and enact through the environment and resources available to the civilisation. McClelland (1951) suggested that external objects become viewed as part of the self when we are able to exercise power or control over them. The screen self is an extension of the self yet detached through its immateriality.

It is worth revisiting Heidegger's articulations about human relation-ships with the technology of 'Being' in the world in its many manifesta-tions. He contends that human beings are themselves reduced to 'standing reserve' or instrumental entities whose purpose is to be used as material to satisfy human need. Heidegger cautions that as long as we see others as standing reserve, and as such immune to violence, power and domination, we become caught in a process of enframing (*Gestell*) whereby we limit our experiences to relationships that render us mere instruments of an economic system (Carey 2000: 26–27). Such a self-enclosing system fore-closes the possibility of ethics while threatening the integrity of life. Heidegger (1993: 246) then calls for people to be seen through their ontological depth rather than being collapsed within the paradigm of enframing. According to Andrew Feenberg, Heidegger demonstrates that 'technology is not merely the servant of some predefined social purpose; it is an environment within which a way of life is elaborated' (p. 127). And thus, 'for good or ill, the human manner of inhabiting the environment can only be [an] ethical' question (cf. Thompson 2000: 206).

BIBLIOGRAPHY

Altheide, D.L. (2000). "Identity and the Definition of the Situation in a Mass-Mediated Context." *Symbolic Interaction, 23*, 1–27.

Bakhtin, Mikhail. (1986). "From Notes Made in 1970–71." *Speech Genres & Other Late Essays.* Translated by Vern W. McGee. Edited by Caryl Emerson and Michael Holquist, 132–58. Austin: U of Texas P.

Baudrillard, Jean. (1983). *Simulations.* New York: Semiotext.

Bauman, Z. (2003). *Liquid Love: On the Frailty of Human Bonds.* Cambridge: Polity.

Beck, U. (2001). *World Risk Society.* Cambridge: Blackwell.

Boltanski, Luc, & Chiapello, Eve. (2002). "The New Spirit of Capitalism", Paper Presented at the Conference of Europeanists, 14–16 March, Chicago, IL.

Bourdieu, P., & Wacquant, L. (1992). *An Invitation to Reflexive Sociology.* Chicago, IL. University of Chicago Press.

Butler, J. (1990). *Gender Trouble: Feminism and the Subversion of Identity.* London and New York: Routledge.

Butler, J. (1991). "Imitation and Gender Insubordination." In *Inside/Out: Lesbian Theories, Gay Theories,* edited by D. Fuss, 13–31. London: Routledge.

Butler, J. (2005). *Giving an Account of Oneself.* New York: Fordham University Press.

Bruner, J. (1997). "The Narrative Model of Self- construction." In *The Self Across Psychology: Self-Recognition, Self-Awareness, and the Self Concept,* edited by J.G. Snodgrass& R.L. Thompson, 145–61. New York: Ann. NY Academy Off Science.

Callero, J. (2003). 'The Sociology of the Self." *Annual Review of Sociology, 29*(2003), 115–133.

Carey, S. (2000). "Cultivating Ethos Through the Body." *Human Studies, 23,* 23–42.

Castells, M. (2000 [1996]). *The Rise of the Network Society* (2nd ed.). Oxford: Blackwell.

Cerulo, Karen A. (1997. "Identity Construction: New Issues, New Directions." *Annual Review of Sociology 23*(1), 385–409.

Coleman, J.S. (1988). "Social Capital in the Creation of Human Capital." *The American Journal of Sociology, 94,* S95–S120 (Supplement).

Cooley, C.H. (1902). *Human Nature and the Social Order*. New York: Scribner.

Cova, B., & Dalli, D. (2009). "Working Consumers: The Next Step in Marketing Theory?" *Marketing Theory, 9*(3), 315–339.

Cover, R. (2012). "Performing and Undoing Identity Online: Social Networking, Identity Theories and the Incompatibility of Online Profiles and Friendship Regimes." *Convergence, 18*(2), 177–193.

Csikszentmihalyi, M., & Rochberg-Halton, E. (1981). *The Meaning of Things: Domestic Symols and the Self*. Cambridge: Cambridge University Press.

Durkheim, E. (1893). 1984. *The Division of Labor in Society*. Beverly Hills, California: Sage.

Dobzhansky, Theodosius. (1964). "Biology, Molecular and Organismic." *American Zoologist*, 443–452.

Donath, J.S., & Boyd, D. (2004). "Public Displays of Connection." *BT Technology Journal, 22*, 71.

Ellison, N.B., Steinfeld, C. & Lampe. C. (2007). "The Benefits of Facebook Friends: Social Capital and College Students' Use of Online Social Network Sites." *Journal of Computer-Mediated Communication, 12*(4), 1143–1168.

Featherstone, Mike, ed. (1988). *Postmodernism. Special Issue of Theory, Culture and Society*. London: Sage.

Foucault, M. (1979). *Discipline and Punish*. New York: Vintage Books.

Foucault, M. (1980). "The Eye of Power." In *Power/Knowledge*, edited by Colin Gordon, 146–165. New York: Pantheon Books, 1980.

Foucault, M. (1988). *The Care of the Self*. New York: Vintage Books.

Giddens, Anthony. (1991). *Modernity and Self-identity: Self and Society in the Late Modern Age*. Cambridge: Polity Press.

Goffman, E. (1959). *The Presentation of Self in Everyday Life*. Garden City, NY: Doubleday Anchor.

Greenblatt, Stephen. (1980). *Renaissance Self- Fashioning: From More to Shakespeare*. Chicago: U of Chicago P.

Granovetter, M.S. (1983). "The Strength of Weak Ties: A Network Theory Revisited." *Sociological Theory, 1*, 201–233.

Gubrium, J.F., & Holstein, J.A. (1995). "Individual Agency, the Ordinary, and Postmodern Life." *The Sociological Quarterly, 36*(3, Summer 1995), 555–570.

Jameson, F. (1985). "Postmodernism and Consumer Society." In *Postmodern Culture*, edited by H. Foster, 111–125. London: Pluto Press.

Haraway, D. (1991). *Simians, Cyborgs and Women: The Reinvention of Nature*. London: Free Association.

Harvey, D. (1990). *The Condition of Post-Modernity*. Cambridge, Oxford: Blackwell.

Hearn, A. (2008). "Meat, Mask, Burden: Probing the Contours of the Branded Self." *Journal of Consumer Culture, 8*(2), 197–217.

Heidegger, M. (1977). "The Age of the World Picture." *The Question Concerning Technology and Other Essays*, 115–154. New York: Harper Torchbooks.

Heidegger, M. (1993). "Letter on Humanism." In *Basic Writings*. Translated by D. Krell. San Fransisco: Harper Collins.

Knorr Cetina, Karin. (2001). "Postsocial Relations: Theorizing Sociality in a Postsocial Environment." In *Handbook of Social Theory*, edited by Barry Smart & George Ritzer. Sage Publications.

Lazzarato, Maurizio (1996). "Immaterial Labor." In *Radical Thought in Italy: A Potential Politics*, edited by Paolo Virno & Michael Hardt, 133–50. Minneapolis, MN and London: University of Minneasota Press.

Levi-Strauss, Claude. (1966). *The Savage Mind*. Chicago: University of Chicago Press.

Lin, N. (1999). Building a Network Theory of Social Capital. *Connections, 22*, 28–51.

Manovich, L. (2001). *The Language of New Media*. Massachussets: MIT Press.

Mead, G.H. (1934). *Mind, Self and Society*. Chicago: University of Chicago.

McClelland, D. (1951). *Personality*. New York: Holt, Rinehart, & Winston.

Meyrowitz, J. (1997). "Shifting Worlds of Strangers: Medium Theory and Changes in "Them" Versus "Us"". *Sociological Inquiry, 67*(1), 59–71.

Mitchell, N.J. (1986). John Locke and the Rise of Capitalism. *History of Political Economy, 18*(2), 291–305.

Prahalad, C.K., & Ramaswamy, V. (2000). "Co-opting Customer Competence." *Harvard Business Review, 78*(1), 79–90.

Portes, A. (1998). "Social Capital: Its Origins and Applications in Modern Sociology." *Annual Review of Sociology, 24*(1), 1–24.

Putnam, R.D. (2000). *Bowling Alone: The Collapse and Revival of American Community*. New York: Simon & Schuster.

Rayner, T. (2001). Biopower and Technology: Foucault and Heidegger's Way of Thinking. Contretemps 2, May 2001; 142–156.

Read, J. (2003). *The Micro-Politics of Capital: Marx and the Prehistory of the Present*. Albany, NY: State University of New York Press.

Resnick, P. (2001). "Beyond Bowling Together: Sociotechnical Capital." In *HCI in the New Millennium*, edited by J. Carroll, 647–672. New York: Addison-Wesley.

Ritzer, G. (2015). "Prosumer Capitalism." *The Sociological Quarterly, 56*(3), 413–445.

Rosenberg, M. (1986). *Conceiving the Self*. Malabar, FL: Krieger Publishing.

Said, Edward W. (1994). "Identity, Authority, and Freedom: The Potentate and the Traveler." *Boundary 2, 21*(3, Fall 1994), 1–18.

Sartre, Jean-Paul. (1974). "The Purpose of Writing." Between Existentialism and Marxism. Translated by John Mathews. New York: Pantheon Books, 1974.

Sawicki, Jana. (1996). "Feminism, Foucault, and 'Subjects' of Power and Freedom." In *Feminist Interpretations of Michel Foucault*, edited by Susan J. Hekman, 159–78. University Park: The Pennsylvania State University Press.

Schieffelin, E.L. (1998). "Problematizing Performance." *Ritual, Performance, Media, 35,* 194.

Steinfield, C., Ellison, N.B., & Lampe, C. (2008). "Social Capital, Self-Esteem, and Use of Online Social Network Sites: A Longitudinal Analysis." *Journal of Applied Developmental Psychology, 29*(6), 434–445.

Taylor, C.T. (1989). *Sources of the Self: The Making of the Modern Identity.* Cambridge, Mass.: Harvard Univ. Press

Terranova, T. (2000). "Free Labor: Producing Culture for the Digital Economy." *Social Text, 18*(2), 33–58.

Thompson, J.B. (1995). *The Media and Modernity: A Social Theory of the Media.* Cambridge: Polity Press.

Thompson, I. (2000). "From the Question Concerning Technology to the Quest for a Democratic Technology: Heidegger, Marcuse, Feenberg." *Inquiry, 43,* 203–16.

Todorov, Tzvetan. (1984). *Dialogical Principle.* Translated by Wlad Godzich. Minneapolis: U of Minnesota P.

Turkle, S. (1995). *Life on the Screen: Identity in the Age of the Internet.* New York: Simon & Schuster.

Vargo, S.L., & Lusch, R.F. (2004). "Evolving to a New Dominant Logic for Marketing." *Journal of Marketing, 68*(1), 1–17.

Van Dijck, J. (2013). "'You have one identity': performing the self on Facebook and LinkedIn." *Media, Culture & Society, 35*(2), 199–215.

Williams, D. (2006). "On and Off the 'Net': Scales for Social Capital in an Online Era." *Journal of Computer-Mediated Communication, 11,* 593–628.

CHAPTER 5

Self and Its 'Strategies for Immortality'

Abstract The online self is one that is acutely aware of the transience of its moral life and its limitations on this earth. Through its disembodied presence online and its ineradicable qualities, the virtual world offers strategies to extend its mortality. Our pull towards the virtual reveals our deep-seated fear of death and the need to place fragments of ourselves to float infinitum as data. Throughout human civilisation, we have sought to retain ourselves on earth through cultural artefacts and, historically, the rich have had more opportunities to do this. The internet, often envisaged as a democratic platform for the masses, offers new ways for recording memory and for renegotiating our ephemeral mortal lives. This chapter discusses our historical anxiety about our morality and mechanisms to sustain our presence in the online environment.

Keywords Death • Immortality • Strategies for Mortality
• Disaster-Selfies • Selfies

INTRODUCTION

Historically, humans have left their mark on the mortal world through different material artefacts connoting varying practices and rituals through time and space. Cultural artefacts ranging from self-portraits to tombstones mark human endeavours to leave traces on this earth where human life is defined by its transience. Our present day 'selfie' culture is examined in this chapter through our obsession with our lack of permanence in the mortal

© The Author(s) 2018   79
Y. Ibrahim, *Production of the 'Self' in the Digital Age*,
https://doi.org/10.1007/978-3-319-74436-0_5

world. Digital modes of living entail not just new practices for now and today but a wider phenomenology that includes a quest to leave traces of ourselves behind. Our human quest for immortality and anxieties over death, I argue, position the internet as a space to enact 'strategies for immortality' (Bauman 1992). With digital space marked through its ineradicable qualities, it resonates with our quest to leave traces of ourselves online, both as data and content, even after our demise. Often our techniques for self-exploration are about the approach of our death, according to Heidegger (cf. Carey 2000: 23). Fear of one's own demise then stimulates the self to engage both in acts of distraction which question the meaning of existence and also strategies to retain the self in the ephemeral world.

The 'selfie' has been an image genre of acute scholarly curiosity in recent times and has elicited different vantage points from the field (see Kuntsman and Stein 2015; Ibrahim 2009; Grabmeier 2015; Fox and Rooney 2015). It has become a common term readily identifiable in popular culture where it is intimately associated with mobile technologies and the digital culture of imaging oneself pervasively. The 'selfie' is an image genre produced by the self with a mobile device such as the smartphone where it collapses the object and subject positions, creating a highly intimate artefact denoting personal ownership. It is equally ascribed through a sense of aesthetics of the self and folds within a wider phenomenon of self-curation, self-representation as well as self-objectification. Personal ownership is juxtaposed with the selfie as a commodity for social exchange and interaction. According to a Pew Study, more than any other generation, millennials aged 18–33 posted selfies, denoting their intense use of the internet, smartphones and social media (Taylor 2014). The study revealed that 55% of this specific age group had posted a selfie on social media sites.

The selfie as a cultural artefact has social resonance in the digital age as it is underpinned through new forms of sociality as well as a communal gaze online. The validation of people's private moments through communal gaze is an important dimension of identity politics in the digital age where the 'selfie' becomes a bigger part of sociality and social transactions online, embedding the act of gazing and sharing in complex ways. The gaze of the known and unknown in this politics of self-objectification implicates different forms of risks and acts of voyeurism and surveillance into this act of sharing the self (Ibrahim 2008a). The selfie culture is also intimately implicated with the accumulation of social capital online. The rituals of inviting others to gaze then validates the self through 'likes' which means that the selfie is fully immersed in an economy of consumption and validation of others. The validation and likes of others is about building and consolidating social capital online. As such the selfie transcends into a politicised entity online pegged to an attention economy while encoding new forms of 'diarisation of the self' through an image genre.

With the convergence of technologies and the embedding of technologies on the body, the selfie captured on a personal gadget can be disseminated and stored online. This ease of capture and dissemination has made the selfie a resonant genre in contemporary culture where it has become part of our ordinary and extraordinary rituals. Mobile technologies and cloud systems that shadow us have become part of a prosthetic memory extending our cognitive function and visuality through their technical capacity. As we seamless fuse bodily pattern, rhythms and temporal pace with technology, technologies as part of our living and breathing body become devices to extend and represent the self in the digital age. The extension of our vision and memory through mobile technologies and convergence have produced an intensity to capture ourselves and our environments, in our static and mobile states. It's not just the ferocity of capture but also our frenetic activity to upload, consume and download through online platforms that means that the self is intimately entwined in this generative economy of gaze and consumption. Our every act and thought lends to this sharing of economy mobile technologies as intimate tools in the narration of everyday life (Ibrahim 2008b, 2015). Compared to film-based photography, digital technologies are associated with immediacy and instant gratification where images can be published and shared with ease.

The incorporation of recording and imaging technologies in smartphones means that the selfie is inserted into a social economy of converting everyday life into modes of sharing and transacting online. New forms of ritual celebrate and memorialise the self in its perfunctory modes. As such the selfie is a distinct cultural genre today, pervasive and generously populated with a click. The selfie as a mode of social exchange and sharing imbues multiple meanings on this genre. For Baudrillard, multiple meanings are produced through symbolic exchanges in postmodernity (cf. Porter 1993: 21). Exchanges of one's images through public and private platforms provide an insight into the human psyche, revealing possibilities and its innermost vulnerabilities in the digital age. Selfies as a genre speak to a multitude of processes online from authentication of life experiences, voyeurism to the invocation of desire. The selfie as part of the re-invention and aestheticization of the self in the digital is layered with visual codes and meanings. As part of a wider image-laden economy online, the selfie occupies an important position in the transcendence of the self from its purely lived moral experience to its resurrection as a screen image and its relationship to a wider economy of data sharing and image abstraction away from its context online. Images as freely abstracted data online that can be stripped from their context means the selfie is subjected to this same displacement on the internet. As such, the social exchange of the selfie is both about the accumulation of meaning as well as its loss online.

The internet, like other technologies that predate it, pledges a popular myth of machines extending life where even if our bodies decompose, our minds and ideas may be unperishable (Brillenburg-Wurth and van de Ven 2012: 52). In locating the selfie as a genre within the image economy of the internet as well as its attendant visuality, the selfie once uploaded is unleashed into a circulatory economy where it can be stripped from its meaning and origins. This viral economy is an unrelenting one where it can conjoin the selfie with unrelated material while imbuing it with an ineradicable immateriality where it can be effaced and morphed into other manifestations. This virality and malleability is part of the circulation economy of the internet. Its ability to absorb and retain matter extracted away from its platforms of production in the bowels of the internet speaks to both our fantasies of empowerment and anxieties about bodily transgressions as image objects online. Digital memory harbours an instability where it has retentive qualities whilst coalescing with its eradicable and malleable elements. Image as part of the data that can be located through search engines, recrafting the selfie as a genre that can be both altered and transgressed through the processes of wider economies of search, gaze and voyeurism. The virtual realm as mediated through the movement of capital and its overriding agenda to monetise and transact data as such remediates the selfie as an unstable cultural artefact.

It would be reductionist to examine the self purely through a capitalist agenda for it would foreclose human agency and creativity enacted through these social and symbolic exchanges of this immaterial form (Baudrillard 1993a, b; Kellner 2006). The selfie needs to be contextualized through the emergent cultures of intense aestheticization and spectacularisation where our social worlds are resurrected through signs and symbols (Baudrillard 1993a). With the advent of social networking sites and the proliferation of profile culture, the resonance of the selfie as a distinct genre marked the self as entering a reciprocal economy of social exchanges. This emphasis on profile culture came to symbolise a complex interplay of sociality, individual agency as well as forms of self-expression and self-representation. In the *Society of Spectacle*, Guy Debord situates individual practices as symbolically important to the production of everyday life and life situations, as people's creative practices are sites of meaning-making and configure in the production of individuality (cf. Best and Kellner 1999: 142–144). For Debord, people reside in a world saturated with images, where lived experiences are substituted with representations. The conversion of direct experiences into spectacle means a commodified self emerges through this spectacularisation of image and its consumption. The objectification of the self where the self has been converted into a commodity for exchange through our own complicity may signal the limit of capitalism. This rendering of self-objectification to capital forces needs nevertheless to be balanced with other symbolic meaning-making and individual agencies that accrue from generating the self through digital modes. Situating the selfie within this creative agency allows other rich meanings and processes to emerge. The self-production in the digital age is ascribed through the hand of capital which does not completely fore-close the digital realm of generativity as sites of symbolic and culture exchange engage the self, its individuation and relationships.

SELF(IE) AS DISASTER PORN

The selfie has taken different permutations over the time since its emergence and appropriation into popular culture. One such sub-genre is the 'disaster selfie' where the self is imaged against the scene and setting of a trauma or disaster. Referred to as the 'disaster selfie' and the genre as 'disaster porn', it depicts the self as composed and constructed through a disaster event and its residual media memory. Postings of such images have invited censure and the moral condemnation of turning disaster sites into sites of pleasure and voyeurism. Numerous instances include selfies posted from the disaster site of Tunisia where 38 people were massacred by a gun-man at a beach resort (Harrold 2015). Similarly, when an earthquake happened in Nepal in May 2015, tourists and onlookers turned the disaster zone into a selfie site (Kanwal 2015). Equally, selfies in grim memorial sites have invited backlash in the public. An 'Auschwitz selfie' by a smiling Alabama teenager during a tour of the Auschwitz concentration camp invoked public wrath and condemnation (Daily Mail 2014).

The selfie becomes a genre of criticism in other social settings and human rituals as well. Despite a long history of photographing the dead in memorial photography (see Meinwald 1990; Fernandez 2011), the selfie has been perceived as a dissonant genre during funeral and death events (Gibbs et al. 2014), highlighting the imaging of death as a modern taboo, particularly through the composition of a selfie. Death is a difficult subject in modernity as the embodied reality of death is displaced through the attention paid to mourners, funeral arrangements and tombstones (Fernandez 2011: 348). In the age of convergence, with the body embedded with digital technologies which can record and capture, the sterility of death and its clinical rituals are disrupted through new norms which have emerged around pervasive imaging. Our ubiquitous recording of our everyday lives has meant a renegotiation of social norms, particularly the boundaries of what could constitute private, public or sacred. These reconfigurations of our social norms invoke questions about taste and decency as well as the ethics and morality about what is taboo and what is acceptable in terms of imaging and sharing on public platforms. The disaster selfie can be considered a limit figure in this politics of ubiquitous imaging and its ensuing morality and ethics.

With broadcasting and mass media, tragic events have been witnessed and narrated through the media. Representing the vantage point of the screen, these 'media events' are often transmitted as seamless narratives by inserting cinematic techniques which pause time and space to centralise these tragic events as moments of national consumption. As part of this technical assemblage, the 'media event' is part of news coverage, which audiences become socialised into. With new media technologies, particularly mobile technologies, the media event has become open-ended, co-opting bystanders who witness through their eyes and technologies simultaneously (Ibrahim 2007, 2011, 2012). Today, with camera phones becoming part of wider event construction, the media event has become an even more unstable phenomenon unleashing different vantage points, unsettling the seamless narratives of the 'media event' previously premised solely through broadcasting and its vantage points of narration. The inclusion of people as witnesses through amateur camera footage has made the disaster event open to public narration through these images and video clips. This production of space through the media event and marathon relays of live broadcasting also produces 'place memory' (see Casey 1997, 186) where these create visual and cartographic resonance with a global audience.

With the production of place memory in the broadcasting and narrating of media events, the disaster selfie emerges as a post-event phenomenon capitalising on the residues of trauma. The disaster selfie as a genre draws on the aura of the disaster while leveraging on its resonance with a wider audience. Hence, its purpose is not about the expression of solidarity but the co-location of the self in that place memory. Drawing on the intertextuality of trauma sites and media events, the disaster selfie claims the backdrop to juxtapose its survival against the inevitability of death and the carnage of disaster. It constantly transgresses the sacredness of life and death and equally counterpoises its existence with the demise of the invisible figures in the backdrop. This juxtaposing of the experiential self against a disaster zone becomes a mechanism to impress its own mortal existence and beam it through media memory. The leveraging of the self through disaster sites again invokes wider questions about the ethics of online visuality and the genre of the disaster selfie.

The complex intertextuality of the disaster selfie needs to be located through the modes of production and the architecture of the internet, particularly the notion of the networked self and the search economy. Entwined through social media networks and search engines, the selfie embeds itself through these viral modes and, as such, disaster sites as media events become a form of social capital in placing them as a backdrop for the selfie. Leveraging on the media event and place memory, the disaster selfie utilises the death or disaster event for its self-curation and aestheticization. In the process, it denigrates human trauma through its exploitative tendencies while embedding and amplifying the self through the architecture of the internet where communal gaze is bound with an attention economy of invisible algorithms and functions of search and retrieval. It then draws attention to what is viral where images and stories can be stripped of their context and origins. The disaster selfie works with this attention economy on the internet while extracting the media event for its own self-curation and for its modes of aestheticization and objectification with a mass audience.

The selfie as a mode of production also thrives on voyeurism where it can reconfigure social norms and boundaries we recognise in the offline world. With its flaneur-like tendencies, the selfie embraces voyeuristic characteristics where danger, disaster and death become props to locate themselves for the consumption of a wider audience. It signifies its ability to transcend from the banal into the extraordinary. As such the selfie is drawn to the abjection of horror to narrate the self rather than relating to the trauma of death and disaster sites. The attraction to the abject is part of our human condition as a resonant aspect of the disaster selfie in terms of its production codes. In the process, our boundaries of sacred and profane are constantly tested in the online environment while highlighting the selfie as a form of popular culture where we may test our own moral and ethical limits in composing the selfie. In the production codes of the disaster selfie, the abject and death are appropriated as props for the performance of the self. The media event becomes a fiction to insert the self into these disaster sites to cross new boundaries in the acts of self-representation and cultural voyeurism. Human tragedy or the loss of lives does not take centre stage in this composition but becomes an intertextual frame to produce resonance with others consuming the self. In our media-saturated and image-laden worlds and as part of a wider consumer society, people are bound up in spectacle and simulacra truncated from an external reality where there is a loss of meaning in the intense spectacularisation of society (see Baudrillard 1983; Kellner 2006). Invoking the moral limits of self-representation, the disaster selfie plays to new codes of production which appease to increasing consumerism while limiting our relationship with social reality.

Selfie and the Abject

Two temporal frames are enfolded into the genre of the selfie: the disaster event and the insertion of the self into a site of abjection as a post-event. The invisibility of carnage, death and disaster are woven into this composition making the abject an integral part of the disaster selfie. Mortal bodies project death as a certainty as mortals must succumb, so argues Roland Barthes (1982: 9). As an embodiment of testimony and history the dead body occupies a contentious space in human civilisation. Forensic science uses dead matter in the form of bones and tissues as evidence to trace microbes and disease; genetics is used to establish the circumstances of what made the body succumb to its demise and to re-trace history and memory (Wolfe 2015: 64; Keenan and Weizman 2012). As such, forensic examinations and specifically osteological analysis can provide vital clues to the archaeology of genocide and other forms of body violence making the dead body a silent political witness to the atrocities of war and horror. The body even in death speaks through these forensic reviews and remains a site of scrutiny where it provides cues and clues to horrors it can no longer verbally communicate. The cadaver presents a 'lacuna' or void between what it experienced and what was articulated on its account (see Agamben 2002). Wolfe (2015: 65) observes that the body of the dead retains the possibility to provide 'a pure externalised, objective reality of memory and experience of trauma' in addressing these voids in testimony. The dead body yields both data and memory through this forensic gaze.

The dead body and the spectacular are entwined intimately. In employing the term 'abjection' Julia Kristeva (1982: 4) terms it as 'that which transgresses borders and boundaries, identity and order, and something which is intrinsic to the human condition'. The Parisian flaneur of the nineteenth century embodies a mobile gaze drawn towards the dead and profane. With the police opening up the Paris morgue to the public in 1864, the revelation of the corpses to the public gaze was an initiative to enable the identification of the dead found in the streets. This opening up of the morgue became an object of public curiosity as opposed to aiding the imperative of the police force (Schwartz 1997; Carney 2010: 20–21). The dead and the spectacular hold a curious bond. In contemporary times, there has been a surge of 'dark tourism' where the touristic enterprise is built on scenes of death, disaster and the macabre (Payne 2015; Stone and Sharpley 2008). Dark tourism relates to 'the presentation and consumption (by visitors) of real and commodified death and disaster sites' (Foley and Lennon 1996: 198). Associated with this is the concept of 'ruin porn' where decay and decomposition of material sites invites the possibilities to re-imagine history through the intimacy of this encounter and to impose renewed moral and rational readings on it (see Vergara 1999; Stoler 2008; Puff 2014). Destruction and ruin become backdrops for the 'selfie', integrating the spectacular as part of our bind with the abject and the dead.

In the long historical trajectory of Western imagination, the concept of ruin has a long-running and complex association, according to Helmut Puff (2014). The aestheticization of destruction has turned ruin into an acceptable and non-threatening configuration (Puff 2014: 19). Our popular culture from news media to science fiction movies exemplify our rapprochement between ruin and disaster. Ruins as a visual representation provide a pause in both temporality and space in symbolic terms. Ruins have a symbolic function where the imaging of slums and decaying urban environments provide a means to renegotiate moral and social boundaries (Vergara 1999). Like the disaster site, the ruin locates the contemporary landscape into wider structures of vulnerability (Stoler 2008: 194). In the process it aestheticizes both decay and abandonment (Puff 2014), entwining abjection and spectacle into an incestuous bind.

Like the notion of ruin, the definitions of the monstrous are grounded in historical notions of abjections encompassing decay, death and bodily wastes (see Kristeva 1982). The power of transgression is inscribed in the abject where it can leap boundaries and categories of logic to destabilise order. For Kristeva (1982: 2), the collapse of meaning is the very location of the abject. It is infused with perverse pleasures and desires, where it draws pleasure from the perverse. The disaster selfie is then about releasing pleasure from the perverse. The genre and its location with the abject draws on disaster, death and bloodshed to compose its existential mortality. In tandem with abjection is the element of voyeurism where the act of looking is conjoined with perversion and desire. The juxtaposition of death and destruction is the perverse pleasure to release its testimony of survival. With the insertion of the disaster selfie as a post-event, it appropriates the phenomenon of post-witnessing where time and space are exploited to curate the self(ie). Themes of survival and the quest to extend the mortal life where others have succumbed become subliminal in this genre of self-imagery.

The phantom presence of death on these portrayals becomes an intertextual frame in these compositions of self-curation and aestheticization. The disaster selfie and the commitment to curate the self against disaster sites is about testing moral and ethical limits of taste and decency in catering to a consumption community. The invocation of death in these self-portraits is about our abject obsession with death in postmodernity. As propounded by Roland Barthes, it is 'neither art nor communication, it is reference' (1982: 76). The disaster selfie becomes part of the performative online where the sacred and profane become interchangeable in composing the self. In postmodernity the collapsing of bounded spheres (i.e. screen and real life), according to Baudrillard (1988: 27), induces 'an over-proximity of all things, a foul promiscuity of all things'. This promiscuous 'hyperreality' is not just about mixing medium and genre but the loss of meaning created through this promiscuous bind. The disaster selfie thwarts the tragic while courting the phantasmagoria of death as its attendant prop to curate itself.

Straddling between perversion, pleasure, voyeurism and abjection, the disaster selfie becomes the limit figure exploiting disaster zones as sites of human trauma to compose itself. Baudrillard (1993a, b) paints postmodernity as increasingly pledged to commodification, which centralises technologies and materiality as dominant modes of cultural production, rendering our mortal lives as further from our human capacities, emotions and qualities. His notion of hyperreality fuses information communication technologies with entertainment, hurling us into experiences that are intense and where codes and structures seek to control our behaviour and thoughts.

These mediations lodge us into new domains of experience, which reconfigure reality and meaning-making. Hyperreality inserts an 'ecstasy of communication' where the subject negotiates proximity to information and images (cf. Kellner 2006). Meaning becomes thwarted and destabilised with our extreme obsession with image and spectacle in our media-saturated worlds. This form of media(ted) consciousness is further augmented through a virulent aestheticization of objects and forms. Baudrillard employs the term 'transaesthetics' to refer to the collapse of bounded spheres of activity such as art where no normative standards may apply in discerning art from object (Baudrillard 1993a, b: 72). The collapsing of meaning also lays siege to our notions of taste where tastes are no longer determinate. In integrating this transaesthetics with the genre of disaster selfie, it functions as a transmuted genre emerging through the media event and self-aesthetics symbolising a space of moral disruption. As an image category it collapses the boundaries between the sacred and profane while thwarting morality and the human capacity to feel empathy and pity.

Elongating Our Mortal Lives

The endeavour to insert the self through the historicity of the media event and disaster sites can be interpreted as part of our 'strategies of immortality' (Bauman 1992) where this quest can encompass bodily and cultural transgressions to elicit attention and conjoin with social memory that outlives us. In *The Pornography of Death*, Geoffrey Gorer (1965) locates sex and death as realms of taboo respectively in the Victorian era and in twentieth century society. Death in the twentieth century is rendered by censure, much like sex in the Victorian era, where it is made non-visible or closeted through euphemisms.

Death is hidden and rendered out of sight in modernity. Both sex and death co-mingle as taboo topics and over time there has been a loosening of strictures from the Middle Ages, according to social historian Philippe Aries (1981: 393). Through time, society has enacted an elaborate architecture of defences such as government, regulations, religion and mortality to guard against the inevitable forces of nature such as ageing and death. Love and death, constituting two weak spots of nature, remain impregnable where 'savage violence always leaked' (Aries 1981: 393). Similarly, others such as Schopenhauer (1966: 463), in his treatise *The World as Will and Representation*, asserts that all 'religions and philosophical systems are designed as an antidote of death'. By restraining death and sexuality through the constraints of taboos and rituals, society sought to subjugate the individual to the collective.

Our unease with death is a resonant part of our human condition in modernity, according to Bauman (1992). Compared to modern times, death was less of an issue in the pre-modern era. Constituted as a daily occurrence which can happen without warning and with frequency, death was not deemed an 'extraordinary event' (1992: 96–97). With the emergence of new ideas about the nature of man and his place in the universe during the Enlightenment, members of a collective (i.e. parishes, families or guilds) gave way to the rise of the individual. This accompanied our obsession with mortality as a centric idea in society (Castano and Dechesne 2005). The project to defeat death is central to modernity. Death was increasingly rendered invisible from daily life and the process of dying became clinical and hidden away from public view to designated places such as the hospital (Fernandez 2011: 354).

The corpse as a shadow that forewarned humans of their transience was banished from the rituals of everyday life, according to Bauman (cf. Jacobsen 2011: 391). Death found its stage in media representation and as abject depictions on the celluloid screen mediated through cinematic techniques. Through media representations death could be banalised and equally become a moral force to inoculate our fears about death (Jacobsen 2011: 392). In modernity, Bauman contends that death is standardised and domesticated such that we can only identify the corpse at a distance, thwarting any serious and intimate encounters with death and 'becoming' a corpse (cf. Fernandez 2011: 356). Death as such enters a realm of entertainment banished from its stark reality.

In his book, *Mortality, Immortality and Other Life Strategies*, Bauman (1992) conceived death as a necessary condition for the emergence of man as a cultural being and for the formation of human cultures. Our awareness of human mortality becomes a driving force for the creation and development of culture (1992: 31). The quest for forms of immortality is a consuming need in humans. While religions can nourish a belief in the afterlife, the symbolic acts of elongating life on earth remains a quest for human kind. Describing this as 'strategies for immortality' these can include passing our genes to our progeny or producing something valuable for humanity (1992: 76–77). The wish to be present in human memory constitutes this earthly mission for an 'ethereal' immortality, where one is immortalised through other people's memory. The knowledge that death is inevitable and the brevity of time is non-negotiable accentuates the anxieties of unfulfilled projects and is the very driving force that propels human imagination into action (Jacobsen 2011: 383).

These strategies for immortality, as Bauman articulates, are 'the principal engine and the flying wheel of cultural creativity and societal survival—and arguably their main raison d'être as well' (cf. Jacobsen 2011: 387). As such his argument is that our strategies to leave our residue and presence in the mortal world can be mediated through class structures and hence the less privileged may not have the means and may be rendered anonymous. Where your individual circumstances do not facilitate the pursuit of immortality, then they may embrace it through collective efforts including nationalist endeavour and ideologies (Castano and Dechesne 2005: 242–243). In contrast to the less privileged, the elites for Bauman (1992: 103) can appropriate 'weapons of self-assertion' to enact a significant and consequential presence in the world. The masses have fewer opportunities in forging and leaving behind a legacy of immortality.

Andrew Keen (2007) through his notion of the 'cult of the amateurs' draws attention to the internet as the demise of the expert and the rise of the layperson or the masses, underscoring the platform as the medium for the masses where user-generated content (UGC) can co-exist with lay knowledge and hence the internet has been a space where professional practices have been reviewed through a romance with the masses. Terms such as citizen journalism and co-creation highlight the platform as amenable for mass humanity. As such, the internet has been re-imagined as a space for extreme creativity and self-expressions embedded through an architecture where data and images can be ineradicable. The conjoining of the digital memory with its storage and circulation economy makes it a viable platform for masses to enact their strategies of immortality. As the self can be performed and consumed by others in different temporal frames through the retentive memory of the digital platform, the personalised mobile screen can be enacted as a tool to address the problem of self and mortality in modernity. This screen culture located through a 'screened reality' of performing the self makes it possible to combine new imaginations of the self as a celebrity through video- and image-sharing platforms. The conjoining of screen culture with UGC and possibilities for celebrification celebrate the internet as a platform for enacting immortality through virality.

The genre of the disaster selfie can be coded as a strategy for immorality in combining public memory with the media event. In modernity the collapsing of spheres and genres creates a confusion rather than an 'ecstasy of communication' through our proximity to images and information in an over-exposed world (Baudrillard 1994: 3). The constitution of the disaster selfie through the genres of selfie and disaster event and its co-mingling with spheres (forms of self-expression and their politics) is both a moment of disruption where our moral boundaries between the sacred and profane are challenged and repositioned. Hence our digital creativity online is defined through this extreme remixing and recombining of different spheres and realms while enacting an attendant proximity to an image-laden world. Such intense repositioning and co-mingling of spheres means that new realms of aestheticization emerge. But, more significantly, it provides humanity with possibilities to renegotiate immortality by the internet as a democratic space for recording, performing and immortalising ordinary lives. In the process, the self can be remorphed in form and meaning online through the digital architecture and its retentive memory.

'SELFIE' AS MEDIATED MEMORY

The internet as a repository of images and data combing individual and communal narratives is a space of memory-making, providing a platform to both re-imagine the individual and collective forms of memorialising such as the imagination of a nation. Durkheim's notion of 'collective consciousness' experienced through the will of a crowd provided the inspiration to Maurice Halbwachs (1992) to posit the notion of collective memory. Cultural tools ignite memory in the individual as part of a member of a group. Despite the act of remembering being a diffused process, cultural artefacts provide an interface between the individual and a wider humanity. Collective memory can be positioned through textual mediation where these become active and symbolic tools to revitalise memory (Wertsch 2006). The selfie is a form of visual mediation and the insertion of the self into historic events provides a means to conjoin the individual to a wider process of memory making that conjoins the wider community. The disaster event, the media event, events that sit outside the realms of the ordinary are opportune moments for the self to cease for the creation of social memory where a wider humanity can locate an unidentified self(ie) to a resonant historic image or encounter.

When conceiving the internet as a space of re-imagination, it can be folded within the paradigm of strategies of immortality where it can help re-mediate social memory through people's everyday life and also conjoin it to wider events. The internet as a platform that enables the residence of people's imagery and narratives enables it to conjoin with the official memory of institutions where it can both substantiate and resist official institutionalised discourses of newspapers, archives and museums or what Finkelstein (2000) terms as the 'Memory Industries'. The telling of individual narratives is not divorced from that of collectivity, according to Frederic Jameson (2013: 49). Personal narratives can be a creative and yet disjunctive form of representation of cultures. As revelatory of individual psyche as well of the ideological forces of nation and culture, they provide forms of textual mediation.

As sites of cultural production, they become spaces of both memory making and self-representation where acts of remembering can manifest through images and through new forms of rituals that emerge online. As a platform that enables private commemoration to be made public, the internet is a hybrid space for renarrating and reviewing history and historicity. Harbouring a multitude of activities, genres and cultural production, the internet is about the mixing of spheres, as Baudrillard (1994) comments in his critique of our image-laden world. This co-mingling can be symbolic of the dialectical struggles of the offline society played out in the online environment. As a space for creativity, creative disruption and for the renegotiation of the sacred, the internet is pregnant with opportunities to resist the linearity of historicity and to induce the self through the historic. New media is equally about the 'emergent' where new rules can be inscribed through new forms of plurality and hybridity of genres online. The reconfiguration of audiences into new modes of production and consumption as well as their enterprise with capitalism online means that the digital platform is about collapsing, fusing and the emergence of new spheres of individual and communal enterprise without decentring our quest for immortality.

The plurality of the internet and its lack of centrality means that it remains a diffused medium filled with fragmentation and divergent agendas. UGC, whether it be selfies, blogs, vlogs or other forms of self-expression, compete for audience attention in the public marketplace of consumption, filled with emergent consumption rituals, which emphasise reciprocity without decentring the self or its obsessions with mortality and the inevitability of death. Our ability to pull the attention of a wider audience is dependent on a complex architecture of search and virality while conceiving the self as a networked entity. As such, self-creation online is welded to a wider economy of content creation and UGC disrupted continuously by emergent consumption and exchange rituals. These peg our social and collective memory to search engines rather than our own recall and in tandem our digital self(ie) online and its association with history is pegged to the ineradicable and search architecture making it both digitally 'memorable' and vulnerable.

SELFIE: THE FLUID AND IMMATERIAL SELF

The politics of identity has emerged as a significant sphere of inquiry. The curation of the self and the quest to sustain an online presence is labour intensive. For Giddens (1991), modern individualism has entailed a move towards a self-based and more self-conscious narrative. The quest for individualism in modernity cultivated through numerous modes of self-expression, including digital platforms, comes at a price. A combination of forces such as capitalism, urbanisation and industrialisation has added to new forms of personal autonomy and individualism on the one hand, but to loneliness, isolation and social fragmentation on the other (Miller et al. 2016: 181). This quest for individualism has been central to Western thought at least since the age of romanticism (Miller et al. 2016: 181). The 'selfie' as a metaphor of our self-obsession in an age of digital photography encompasses both our anxieties and our increasingly networked individualism where the self becomes a life project of self projection. The pledging of the self to the digital economy and its virulent circulation means the online self is co-produced through a convergent and circulatory economy dependent on the gaze, reciprocity and the voyeur of the internet. Stripped from the body and recast as an immaterial entity, the selfie as a genre of production reveals the quest to possess a presentational self online and ironically its recurrent obsession with an 'authentic self' while negotiating between a corporeal presence offline and an immaterial presence online. The immaterial selfie, while celebrating individualism, is a networked entity tightly regulated through digital platforms of interactivity.

The genre of the selfie is here to stay. The selfie as a form of digital self-image was born through the convergence of digital technologies and equally the extension of the senses through mobile telephony and ubiquitous computing, which became embedded onto the corporeal body. The human looking at the self as it goes through its life—both banal and extraordinary—situates the selfie as a form of image diary manufactured to validate life experiences and communicate these with others as a means of producing social memory through a collective gaze. The selfie or the visual diarisation of the self, taps into a very primordial curiosity about the self as a visual entity. Unlike the mirror, the selfie is made for both spectatorship and private pleasures. The selfie as an autoscopic experience is about moving beyond the visualisation of the self through technologies and about casting the self into new modes of circulation, sharing, aestheticization as well as new forms of anxieties afforded through the networked economy of image and content sharing, tagging and voyeurism. Here the gaze can be visualised through the interactivity of the platforms and the ability to track the metrics of the digital platform. There is a general acknowledgement that there is pleasure in looking or, to use Freud's term, 'scopophilia'. The importance of the gaze in society and its relationship to subjectivity is echoed by Lacan who argues that the gaze is a primary part of human subjectivity. For Lacan the gaze extends into the social and imaginary from the real. From a Lacanian perspective, analysis of the gaze can be useful for understanding more about the visual dimension of power, gender and subjectivity in human cultures.

The embedding of new media technologies on the body reframes our sense of sociality and loneliness in modernity where image cultures and the notion of self-curation seek to negotiate a relationship with a visual online self. Characterised through its immateriality, used as a form of reciprocation and yet amenable to both the congenial and hostile gaze of others, the self(ie) is a contested visual entity embodying both exhibitionistic elements and the vulnerabilities produced by the flaming and gaze cultures of the internet and social media. This screen, which is our new mode of sociality, allows the self to be consumed by others affording it a transaction value as well as reciprocity in communication and in asserting a sense of presence online. Presence and transaction value recode the selfie as cultural artefact and equally a tool of self-expression.

The immaterial self 'doubled' through autoscopic encounters enables a reframing of both the temporal and spatial dimensions where the self can inhabit different spaces and temporal frames while living out its everyday life. The self and its everyday existence are afforded a transcendental value through the screen where it can be re-enacted through new aesthetic modes and practices. This renewed aesthetics of the everyday is vital for not only does it locate our fragmented lives through the stability of the everyday but the screen now enables new forms of communion and sociality by centring the self as a source of performance. Within our accelerated modernity where speed becomes an element of living and working, the intrusion into the everyday and its re-performance through the screen in some ways brings into scrutiny how we celebrate the gaze into the ordinary against this Virillian accelerated modernity. Speed and the banal start to coexist while inscribing and obliterating the time of the everyday.

Despite its disembodiment, the selfie has ironically brought the body to the forefront of image cultures online and this reassertion is seen as exerting different forms of social pressure and self-censure in reproducing ourselves online. New forms of harm and risk emerge for young users in particular and where co-presence is established through visual communication on platforms like Snapchat (see McLean et al. 2015). The immaterial and visualised body online is a site of intense identity politics conjoined to a wider economy of UGC and our unfolding anxieties in modernity where the screen is a space for watching and inserting the self. The curation of the immaterial self online imposes immense pressure on the lived self and in the process a whole set of conventions and material practices have emerged around selfie culture. As such, selfie culture cannot be premised through narcissistic tendencies alone but also through a prosumer economy and the social exchanges it facilities by transacting something as personal as a selfie on a public platform. The ubiquitous imaging of the self then poses new ethical and moral challenges on what is acceptable. The act of watching is doubled both through the corporeal body and through the lens and 'vision' of the screen. This doubling of the self and its travel online entails human labour and commitment to curate the self and its presence online. The immateriality of the digital environment means that the self has an unstable mutation as a visual image. The digital image can be altered or photoshopped and through the use of light or filters the image enters realms of aesthetic refinement. This altered image then straddles the discourse of being 'authentic' online, giving rise to new forms of neurosis about appearing authentic on-screen.

What is less conceptualised in the selfie economy is the notion of self-gaze which becomes a means to re-assess the self and its sense of presence and aesthetics in the wider digital economy and equally in terms of 'life' offline. This self-gaze is not autonomous as it draws constantly from the conventions of its presence and practices offline and online and equally it draws on its receptivity by others. This self-gaze as such can be self-regulating and produces incessant vulnerabilities. This again brings the concept of 'authenticity' to the forefront as the self is constantly judged through an intangible quality on which society places an enormous value. The self as a published entity and an entity reframed through 'publicness' constantly lives and works through forms of public gaze and conventions that have emerged online with the exhibition of the self. This public gaze is remediated through its own self-censure and as such the online self is a highly regulated entity. The ability to be captured with ease is mediated through an environment where the gaze of others can regulate us and bring new forms of social pressures, pleasures, desires, voyeurism and anxieties framing the selfie as a promiscuous entity.

The screen doubling of self and its immateriality calls for new ways to understand the selfie as modes of practice where there are renewed investments in the self as a published entity with a presence on digital platforms. Secondly, the new modes of technological-sociality mean that the self and its visuality are facilitated through forms of interactivity and participation of others in this co-production. Equally, it reiterates the immaterial self as a 'staged self' as it captures a moment in time that is meant to be shared with others (Peek 2014). The selfie as a predominant genre on social media is evident through its rising statistic. In 2015, 74% of all images shared on Snapchat were selfies (Cohen 2016). The staging of the self and participation of others means that value is enacted through this co-enterprise and the formation of social capital is through the act of sharing in a networked economy. As such self-curation goes through a process of refinements and reinventions in catering to a known and unknown gaze underpinning the salience of sharing and a viral economy that relentlessly circulates content online. Entering a consumption economy, the self is simultaneously a subject and object, which can be branded and drafted into consumerist economies where it can be promoted and become content for advertising. The selfie as a cultural form is inserted into modes of production, commodification and aestheticization.

The visualised self is an entity that has engaged with the materiality of its environment to reproduce itself. To leave marks and imagery has been a persistent pre-condition of the anxieties around death and mortality. The expressive utilisation of the environment to leave reproductions of ourselves and equally on the memory of others who bear witness to our lives mean that the self has always shared a contentious relationship with time and the temporal framing of mortality. Hence the diarisation of the self through narratives and visual montages is part of the affirmation of its reality and existence on earth where the recording of the ageing body and its relationship with time affords new means to understand the selfie as a significant tool in marking the passage of time and its experiential moments crafted through an image economy. The fluidity of the digital self is marked through its ability to travel and occupy multiple spaces online, simultaneously—a feat not feasible for the offline self. The online spaces roll out time differently where people and life can be on display infinitum. Digital living marks out time differentially, enabling the temporal frames from different spaces to coalesce and facilitate transactions and interactions without restrictions. This notion of digital spaces as always open and amenable to interactivity captures modernity's quest to fill lonely hours with new modes of activity but equally to enter into transactions and sociality that will hinge and valorise both self-gaze and the gaze of others through a digital visuality where the self becomes a visualised life project.

BIBLIOGRAPHY

Agamben, Georgio. (2002). *Remnants of Auschwitz: The Witness and the Archive.* New York: Zone.

Aries, P. (1981). *The Hour of Our Death.* Translated by Helen Weaver. New York: Alfred A. Knopf. 393.

Barthes, R. (1982). *Camera Lucida.* Translated by Richard Howard. London: Jonathan Cape Ltd.

Baudrillard, J (1983). *In the Shadow of the Silent Majorities.* New York: Semiotext(e).

Baudrillard, J. (1988). *America.* London: Verso.

Baudrillard, J. (1993a). *The Transparency of Evil.* London: Verso.

Baudrillard, J. (1993b). *Symbolic Exchange and Death.* London: Sage.

Baudrillard, J. (1994). *Simulacra and Simulation.* Ann Arbor: The University of Michigan Press.

Bauman, Z. (1992). *Mortality, Immortality and Other Life Strategies.* Cambridge: Polity Press.

Bauman, Z. (2013). *Liquid Modernity.* John Wiley & Sons.

Best, S., & Kellner, D. (1999). "Debord, Cybersituationists and the Interactive Spectacle." *Substance, 28*(3), 129–156.

Brillenburg-Wurth, K., & van de Ven, I. (2012, May). "Posthumously Speaking: Thanatography in a Posthuman Age." *Frame, 25*(1). http://www.tijdschriftframe.nl/25-1-narrating-posthumanism/kiene-brillenburg-wurth-and-inge-van-deven-posthumously-speaking-thanatography-in-a-posthuman-age/.

Carey, S. (2000). "Cultivating Ethos Through the Body." *Human Studies, 23,* 23–42.

Carney, P. (2010). "Crime, Punishment and the Force of the Photographic Spectacle." In *Framing Crime: Cultural Criminology and the Image,* edited by K. Hayward, and M. Presdee, 17–35. Abingdon, Oxon: Routledge.

Casey, Edward. (1997). *Remembering: A Phenomenological Study.* Bloomington: Indiana University Press.

Castano, E., & Dechesne M. (2005). "On Defeating Death: Group Reification and Social Identification as Immortality Strategies." *European Review of Social Psychology*, *16*, 221–255.

Cohen, D. (2016, January). "Which Was More Deadly in 2015: Shark Attacks, or Selfies? The Answer Might Surprise You." *Adweek*. http://www.adweek.com/digital/rawhide-selfies-infographic/.

Debord, G. (1967). *The Society of Spectacle*. Detroit: Black and Red.

Fasick, K., Jamieson, A., & Harshbarger, R. (2015, March 29). "Heartless Visitors Mug for Selfies at East Village Blast Site." *New York Post*. http://nypost.com/2015/03/29/heartless-jerks-snap-selfies-at-east-village-blast-site/.

Fausing, B. Become an Image. On Selfies, Visuality and the Visual Turn in Social Medias, KEY NOTE, Rome 1.11.2013.

Fernandez, I. (2011). "The Lives of Corpses: Narratives of the Image in American Memorial Photography." *Mortality, 16*(4), 343–364.

Finklestein, N. (2000). *The Holocaust Industry: Reflections on the Exploitation of Jewish Suffering*. London: Verso.

Foley, M., & Lennon J. (1996). "JFK and Dark Tourism: A Fascination with Assassination." *International Journal of Heritage Studies*, *2*, 198–211.

Fox, J., & Rooney, M.C. (2015). "The Dark Triad and Trait Self-Objectification as Predictors of Men's Use and Self-Presentation Behaviors on Social Networking Sites." *Personality & Individual Differences, 76*, 161–165.

Freud, S. (1905). "Three Essays on the Theory of Sexuality." In *The Standard Edition of the Complete Psychological Works of Sigmund Freud*, gen. edited and translated by James Strachey, vol. 7, 156–157. London: Hogarth, 1986.

Gibbs, M., Nansen, B., Carter, M., & Kohn, T. (2014). "Selfies at Funerals: Remediating Rituals of Mourning." In *The 15th Annual Meeting of the Association of Internet Researchers*. Daegu, Korea, 22–24 October 2014.

Giddens, A. (1991). *Modernity and Self-Identity: Self and Society in the Late Modern Age*. Cambridge: Polity.

Gorer, G. (1965). *Death, Grief, and Mourning in Contemporary Britain*. London: Cressset.

Grabmeier, J. (2015, January 6). *Hey Guys, Posting a Lot of Selfies Doesn't Send a Good Message*. The Ohio State University. https://news.osu.edu/news/2015/01/06/hey-guys-posting-a-lot-of-selfies-doesn%E2%80%99t-send-a-good-message/.

Halbwachs, M. (1992). *On Collective Memory. Translation of Les Cadres Sociaux de la Mémoire*. Edited, translated and with an introduction by Lewis A. Coser. Chicago: University of Chicago Press.

Hansen, S. (2013). "Julia Kristeva and the Politics of Life." *Journal of French and Francophone Philosophy – Revue de la philosophie française et de langue française, XXI*(1), 27–42.

Harrold, A. (2015, June 29). "Labour Candidate Amran Hussain Defends Selfie-Stick Picture on Beach Where Tunisian Massacre...." *The Independent*. http://www.msn.com/en-gb/news/uknews/labour-candidate-amran-hussain-defends-selfie-stick-picture-on-beach-where-tunisian-massacre/ar-AAch5ZX?ocid=UP97DHP.

Jameson, F. (2013). *The Political Unconscious: Narrative as a Socially Symbolic Act*. Routledge.

'I Wouldn't Do Anything Differently': Teen Who Took Selfie at Auschwitz Is Unrepentant as Trend for Grinning and Pouting Poses at Memorials Including Ground Zero Grows. *Daily Mail*. (2014, July 23). http://www.dailymail.co.uk/news/article-2702161/I-wouldnt-differently-Teenager-took-selfie-Auschwitz-unrepentant-trend-posing-memorials-including-Ground-Zero-grows.html.

Keen, A. (2007). *The Cult of the Amateur: How Today's Internet Is Killing Our Culture*. New York: Doubleday.

Keenan, Thomas, & Eyal Weizman. (2012). *Mengele's Skull: The Advent of Forensic Aesthetics*. London: Sternberg Press.

Ibrahim, Y. (2007). "The Technological Gaze: Event Construction and the Mobile Body." *M/C Journal, 10*(1). http://journal.media-culture.org.au/0703/03-ibrahim.php.

Ibrahim, Y. (2008a). "The New Risk Communities: Social Networking Sites and Risk." *International Journal of Media and Cultural Politics, 4*(2), 245–253.

Ibrahim, Yasmin. (2008b). "The Co-opted Body and Counter-Surveillance: The Body as Data and Surveillance." *International Journal of the Humanities, 5*(12), 1–8.

Ibrahim, Y. (2009). "Social Networking Sites (SNS) and the 'Narcissistic Turn'." *Collaborative Technologies and Applications for Interactive Information Design: Emerging Trends in User Experiences: Emerging Trends in User Experiences, 82*.

Ibrahim, Yasmin. (2011). "The Non-Stop 'Capture': The Politics of Looking in Postmodernity." *The Poster, 1*(2), 167–185.

Ibrahim, Yasmin. (2012). "The Politics of Watching: Visuality and the New Media Economy." *International Journal of E-Politics (IJEP), 3*(1), 1–11.

Ibrahim, Y. (2015). "Instagramming Life: Banal Imaging and the Poetics of the Everyday." *Journal of Media Practice, 16*(1).

Jacobsen, M. (2011). "Sociology, Mortality and Solidarity. An Interview with Zygmunt Bauman on Death, Dying and Immortality." *Mortality, 16*(4), 380–393.

Kanwal, R. (2015, May 1). "Disaster Selfies, Treasure Scavengers and Saviours from the Sky: Stories of Heroism and Tragedy in the Aftermath of Nepal's Killer Earthquake." *The Daily Mail*. http://www.dailymail.co.uk/indiahome/indianews/article-3064702/Disaster-selfies-tourists-turned-reliefworkers-saviours-sky-Stories-heroism-tragedy-aftermath-Nepal-s-killer-earthquake.html.

Kristeva, J. (1982). *Powers of Horror, An Essay on Abjection*. New York: Columbia University Press.

Kellner, D. (2006). "Jean Baudrillard After Modernity: Provocations on a Provocateur and Challenger." *International Journal of Baudrillard Studies*, *1*(3). http://www.ubishops.ca/baudrillardstudies/vol3_1/kellner.htm.

Kuntsman, A., & Stein, R.L. (2015). *Digital Militarism: Israel's Occupation in the Social Media Age*. Stanford University Press.

Lacan J. (1998). *The Seminar of Jacques Lacan, Book XI: The Four Fundamental Concepts of Psychoanalysis*. Edited by Jacques-Alain Miller. Translated by Alan Sheridan. New York and London: Norton, 1977.

McLean, S. A., Paxton, S. J., Wertheim, E. H., & Masters, J. (2015). "Photoshopping the Selfie: Self Photo Editing and Photo Investment Are Associated with Body Dissatisfaction in Adolescent Girls." *International Journal of Eating Disorders*, 48(8), 1132–1140.

Meinwald, Dan. (1990). *Memento Mori: Death and Photography in 19th-Century America*. Riverside, CA: CMP Bulletin, vol. *9*(4). http://cmp1.ucr.edu/terminals/memento_mori.

Miller, Daniel, Costa, Elisabetta, Haynes, Nell, McDonald, Tom, Nicolescu, Razvan, Sinanan, Jolynna, Spyer, Juliano, Venkatraman, Shriram, & Xinyuan, Wang. (2016). "Individualism." In *How the World Changed Social Media*, 181–92. London: UCL Press. http://www.jstor.org/stable/j.ctt1g69z35.19.

Payne, E. (2015, March 5). "Trips to Disaster Sites Where Rescuers Are Still Retrieving Bodies, Tours of Fukushima and Selfies During the Sydney Siege: The Ominous Rise of Dark Tourism." *The Daily Mail*. http://www.dailymail.co.uk/travel/travel_news/article-2979053/Trips-disaster-sites-rescuers-retrieving-bodies-tours-Fukushima-selfies-Sydney-siege-ominous-rise-dark-tourism.html.

Peek, H. (2014). "The Selfie in the Digital Age: From Social Media to Sexting." *Psychiatric Times, 31*(12), 28.

Porter, R. (1993). "Baudrillard: History, Hysteria and Consumption." *Forget Baudrillard*, 1–21.

Puff, Helmut. (2014). *Miniature Monuments: Modelling German History*. Berlin: Walter de Gruyter.

Schwartz, V.R. (1997). *Spectacular Realities: Early Mass Culture in fin-de-siècle Paris*. University of California Press.

Schopenhauer, Arthur. (1966). "On Death and Its Relation to the Indestructibility of Our Inner Nature." In *The World as Will and Representation*, vol. II. Translated by E.F.J. Payne. New York: Dover.

Stoler, Ann Laura, (2008). "Imperial Debris: Reflections on Ruins and Ruination." *Cultural Anthropology, 23*, 192–194.

Stone, P., & Sharpley, R. (2008). "Consuming Dark Tourism: A Thanatological Perspective." *Annals of Tourism Research, 35*(2), 574–595.

Taylor, P. (2014, March 4). "More Than Half the Millennials Have Shared a Selfie." *Pew Research Centre.* http://www.pewresearch.org/fact-tank/2014/03/04/more-than-half-of-millennials-have-shared-a-selfie/.

Vergara, Camilo José. (1999). *American Ruins.* New York: Monacelli Press.

Wertsch, J.V. (2006). "Narrative as a Cultural Tool in Collective Memory." In *Conference for Sociocultural Research III,* 2000. 9 September 2006. http://www.fae.unicamp.br/br2000/trabs/2045.doc.

Wolfe, E. (2015). "Speaking the Lacuna: The Archaeology of Plantation Slavery as Testimony." *Digital Literature Review, 2,* 63–74.

INDEX

© The Author(s) 2018
Y. Ibrahim, *Production of the 'Self' in the Digital Age*,
https://doi.org/10.1007/978-3-319-74436-0